Google Apps Script for Beginners

Customize Google Apps using Apps Script and explore its powerful features

Serge Gabet

PUBLISHING

BIRMINGHAM - MUMBAI

Google Apps Script for Beginners

First published: February 2014

Production Reference: 1140214

Published by Packt Publishing Ltd.
Livery Place
35 Livery Street
Birmingham B3 2PB, UK.

ISBN 978-1-78355-217-7

www.packtpub.com

Cover Image by Glen Michael Carrie (glen.m.carrie@gmail.com)

Credits

Author
Serge Gabet

Reviewers
Henrique Abreu
David Bingham
Alejandro Leiva
Rohit Mukherjee
Ajith Ranabahu

Acquisition Editor
Kevin Colaco

Content Development Editor
Shaon Basu

Technical Editors
Mrunal Chavan
Sebastian Rodrigues

Copy Editors
Tanvi Gaitonde
Insiya Morbiwala
Stuti Srivastava

Project Coordinator
Harshal Ved

Proofreaders
Simran Bhogal
Stephen Copestake

Indexer
Monica Ajmera Mehta

Production Coordinator
Nitesh Thakur

Cover Work
Nitesh Thakur

About the Author

Serge Gabet has been a professional audio equipment manufacturer for 20 years and is now working for an artistic upper school in Brussels, Belgium as a teacher and Technical Manager. He is also in charge of the Google Apps administration of this school. He develops custom applications using Google Apps Script mainly for his school, though he also works in other areas.

He has been designated a Top Contributor by Google since June 2011. He was active on the Google Group Help forum till 2012, then on the Stack Overflow forum (the Google Help Group forum was closed in June 2012), and became a first ranker and an all-time contributor on the Stack Overflow forum a few months back.

I'd like to thank all the forum contributors who were on the same forum at the time that I was new to the forum and helped me take my first steps. Most of them are now Top Contributors too and even if their knowledge was (and still is) greater than mine, they never make me feel it. Thanks for that.

Also, thanks to Google collaborators for their day-to-day presence and for listening to our concerns.

About the Reviewers

Henrique Abreu is a Google Apps Script Top Contributor; he graduated in Control Engineering and works as an IT consultant in Brazil. He is a big fan of Google Apps, especially Spreadsheets and of course, Apps Script.

David Bingham has been developing software and leading product development teams for more than 25 years, with a side trip into academia as a professor of Computer Architecture. He is currently working as an R&D leader for a global provider of Unified Communications and Collaboration software. In his spare time, he enjoys travelling and spending time with his family. His alter ego, Mogsdad, is an active contributor to the Google Apps Script community.

Alejandro Leiva has been using computers with modems of 600 bps connected to pre-Internet networks were used, since the age of 12. He has been working in the areas of software development, technical leadership, project management, and building an executive profile where he temporarily needed to switch his development framework for a spreadsheet and choose Google Apps Scripts as his new language. He has excellent skills in technical team building, agile environments, open source software development and accessibility. His Twitter handle is @gloob.

Thanks to my supportive wife and especially my beloved daughter for bringing new energy into my life.

Rohit Mukherjee is currently studying Computer Engineering at the National University of Singapore (NUS) on a full scholarship offered by Singapore Airlines (SIA-NOL). He is passionate about Software Engineering, Linux, Dev Ops, Agile Methodologies, and Technology Startups. He is interested in the fields of financial and healthcare technologies. He is currently studying graduate courses in computer science as an exchange student at ETH Zurich. For more information, visit his web page rohitmukherjee.github.io.

Rohit works as an independent software developer and has pursued an industrial interest with The Bank of America Merrill Lynch (Singapore). He has also interned with Ernst & Young, India and Klinify, Singapore in the past. He is a contributor to open source software as well.

I would like to thank my parents for their support.

Ajith Ranabahu is an experienced software engineer and an avid open source enthusiast. He holds a PhD in Computer Science and is a member of the Apache Software Foundation. He has contributed heavily to the Apache Axis2 project and a number of other small projects over the years.

www.PacktPub.com

Support files, eBooks, discount offers, and more

You might want to visit www.PacktPub.com for support files and downloads related to your book.

Did you know that Packt offers eBook versions of every book published, with PDF and ePub files available? You can upgrade to the eBook version at www.PacktPub.com and as a print book customer, you are entitled to a discount on the eBook copy. Get in touch with us at service@packtpub.com for more details.

At www.PacktPub.com, you can also read a collection of free technical articles, sign up for a range of free newsletters and receive exclusive discounts and offers on Packt books and eBooks.

http://PacktLib.PacktPub.com

Do you need instant solutions to your IT questions? PacktLib is Packt's online digital book library. Here, you can access, read and search across Packt's entire library of books.

Why subscribe?

- Fully searchable across every book published by Packt
- Copy and paste, print and bookmark content
- On demand and accessible via web browser

Free access for Packt account holders

If you have an account with Packt at www.PacktPub.com, you can use this to access PacktLib today and view nine entirely free books. Simply use your login credentials for immediate access.

Table of Contents

Preface

A couple of years ago, I was asked by a colleague to create a form to collect invitation responses for a show that our school was organizing. Like most computer users, I had some experience with spreadsheets and had used them from time to time to do some basic calculations, so I created a form with the results in a spreadsheet.

At this point, I simply wanted to count the responses and show the result somehow. As I didn't know how to get a clear view of these results and a simple addition of numbers was not very attractive to look at, I decided to take a quick peek at the documentation to see how to write a "macro" to eventually get things to look better.

Three days later, the spreadsheet had a custom menu. It had functions that showed me the results in colorful tables and sent me an e-mail when too many people had made a reservation for the same day.

I discovered that this "macro" that I was looking for had a lot more features than that; I had a whole bunch of tools and services that I was able to customize exactly to what I needed, without spending a single cent on it.

This was the end of my "peaceful life without Google Apps Script" and the beginning of a real adventure. I didn't know a single word of JavaScript or HTML. My only programming experience was using BASIC on an 8-bit microcomputer from the 1980s, so I knew that there would be a few things to learn.

This happened in 2009. At the time, Google Apps Script was just beginning its development. As it has grown a lot since then, it has provided an opportunity for my skills to improve as well. At that time, I found help from a couple of guys on the Google group help forum (now closed and wiped out). Thanks Henrique, scampmichael, and velosprinter—they know who they are.

I know that each of us has a different background and follows a different path but, nevertheless, I decided to present this book following the same progression that I had followed—from basic spreadsheet enhancement and customization to standalone web apps with really powerful features. In between, we shall see that other documents can have embedded scripts and that most of the Google services can communicate with Google Apps Script.

There is probably no way to present every possible combination of scripts and methods that are available exhaustively in a single book. But, I'll try to pick up the most useful and interesting ones based on what I see every day on the well-known help site where I participate a lot: `http://stackoverflow.com/questions/tagged/google-apps-script`.

What this book covers

Chapter 1, Enhancing Spreadsheets, is an introduction to JavaScript as a spreadsheet macro language. It shows you how many aspects of a spreadsheet document could be modified using Google Script—not only layout and formatting but sharing and publishing as well.

Chapter 2, Create and Manipulate Forms, deals with an automated form creation and modification with Google Apps Script. It demonstrates the ability of forms to respond to triggers, thereby automatically sending an evaluation with reference to good and bad answers.

Chapter 3, Managing an E-mail Account, shows you how to send messages, filter your messages, and combine Gmail with documents to create your own workflow. You will learn that Google service offers an impressive panel of methods that allows for almost any possible manipulation of your mailbox content.

Chapter 4, Embedding Scripts in Text Documents, shows you how to build and analyze Google documents using JavaScript. You will also see how to build or change a document's content and how to analyze what is already present in the document.

Chapter 5, Embedding Scripts in Google Sites, demonstrates how a script updates your Google site automatically. This chapter also demonstrates the multiple aspects and advantages of the communication and combination of multiple services.

Chapter 6, Standalone Web Applications / User Interfaces, teaches you how to create web applications that work everywhere and that anyone can use. It also shows you how to protect your private data across the Internet.

Chapter 7, Using User Interfaces in Spreadsheets and Documents, empowers you to use your new skills to create more user-friendly documents and worksheets. It will simplify your work with spreadsheets and documents to either show data in a way that is not directly available or to add extra functionalities.

Chapter 8, How to Expand Your Knowledge, gives you tips and tricks to learn what this book could not cover. It will give you an overview of the many resources available to help improve your learning experience.

Chapter 9, Conclusion, ends with perspectives, secrets, and the author's personal point of view.

What you need for this book

You need only an Internet connection and a modern browser, although any browser should work without restriction. As most of the code is executed on a distant server, some rendering may differ if you use an old version of Microsoft Internet Explorer.

I would recommend you to use Google Chrome as it will automatically offer you one of the best compatibility performances and updates.

Besides that, you won't have to install anything.

Who this book is for

Do you like the idea of having some tasks executed automatically for you and want to get things done more simply? That's exactly the purpose of this book.

You won't need any preliminary knowledge to start reading, but be prepared to learn a lot of things in a short time. Being comfortable with basic text writing and manipulation such as copy and paste are mandatory requests.

Conventions

In this book, you will find a number of styles of text that distinguish between different kinds of information. Here are some examples of these styles, and an explanation of their meaning.

Code words in text, database table names, folder names, filenames, file extensions, pathnames, dummy URLs, user inputs, and Twitter handles are shown as follows: "As you can notice, we use `#name#` to mark the placeholders."

A block of code is set as follows:

```
var docCopy = DriveApp.getFileById(sharedDocID).makeCopy('menu['+heade
rs[todayInSheet]+']');
  menuFolder.addFile(docCopy);
  DriveApp.getRootFolder().removeFile(docCopy);
```

When we wish to draw your attention to a particular part of a code block, the relevant lines or items are set in bold:

```
function myAgeInHours(){
  var myBirthDate = new Date('1958/02/19 02:00:00').getTime();
  myBirthDate = parseInt(myBirthDate/3600000, 10);
```

New terms and **important words** are shown in bold. Words that you see on the screen, in menus or dialog boxes for example, appear in the text like this: "Open the script editor from the **Tools** menu and write the code snippet we just prepared.".

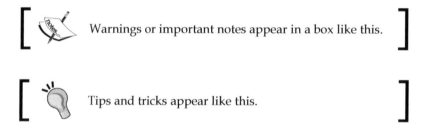

Warnings or important notes appear in a box like this.

Tips and tricks appear like this.

Reader feedback

Feedback from our readers is always welcome. Let us know what you think about this book—what you liked or may have disliked. Reader feedback is important for us to develop titles that you really get the most out of.

To send us general feedback, simply send an e-mail to feedback@packtpub.com, and mention the book title through the subject of your message.

If there is a topic that you have expertise in and you are interested in either writing or contributing to a book, see our author guide on www.packtpub.com/authors.

Customer support

Now that you are the proud owner of a Packt book, we have a number of things to help you to get the most from your purchase.

Downloading the example code

You can download the example code files for all Packt books you have purchased from your account at http://www.packtpub.com. If you purchased this book elsewhere, you can visit http://www.packtpub.com/support and register to have the files e-mailed directly to you.

Errata

Although we have taken every care to ensure the accuracy of our content, mistakes do happen. If you find a mistake in one of our books — maybe a mistake in the text or the code — we would be grateful if you would report this to us. By doing so, you can save other readers from frustration and help us improve subsequent versions of this book. If you find any errata, please report them by visiting http://www.packtpub.com/support, selecting your book, clicking on the **errata submission form** link, and entering the details of your errata. Once your errata are verified, your submission will be accepted and the errata will be uploaded to our website, or added to any list of existing errata, under the Errata section of that title.

Piracy

Piracy of copyright material on the Internet is an ongoing problem across all media. At Packt, we take the protection of our copyright and licenses very seriously. If you come across any illegal copies of our works, in any form, on the Internet, please provide us with the location address or website name immediately so that we can pursue a remedy.

Questions

You can contact us at questions@packtpub.com if you are having a problem with any aspect of the book, and we will do our best to address it.

1
Enhancing Spreadsheets

Spreadsheets are probably the favorite entry point for any future Google Apps Script user; their primary use is to process data one way or another.

A Google spreadsheet has the basic features of all spreadsheets, using a grid of cells arranged in numbered rows and letter-named columns to organize data manipulations.

The major differences compared to other spreadsheets are that it opens in a generic browser without needing any specific program installation or license and all the data processing is handled outside your computer on Google's servers.

It is also shareable among any number of users in real time as long as they have an Internet connection and it doesn't need to be saved because every single-cell edit is recorded seamlessly and every change is logged in a so-called revision history (accessible from the **File** menu) that allows you to recover any previous version while being able to see who made the change and when.

When Google introduced this spreadsheet service back in 2006 as an experimental feature, I found it attractive because of the shareable access and also because cloud-based applications were new and seemed a bit magical. Now that almost everything can be hosted in the cloud, the magic has gone; nevertheless, it's still very comfortable to use.

Spreadsheet functions versus Google Apps Script – how to choose?

As mentioned before, spreadsheets are capable of performing all sorts of operations, from math to string manipulation and resolving complex financial formulas.

To be convinced of its interest, you just have to take a look at the drive help page or simply type = in a spreadsheet followed by any letter (for example, *S*) and you get a list of all the spreadsheet functions whose names start with the letter *S* (`https://support.google.com/drive/table/25273?hl=en`) as shown in the following screenshot:

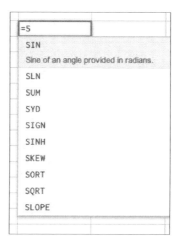

These functions are built into the spreadsheet; they can be put together and combined in many ways. They also execute pretty fast and most of them are compatible with other spreadsheet formats such as Microsoft Excel or Apache OpenOffice such that they will continue working if ever you download the document for any reason. That's undoubtedly an advantage and most of the functions have names that are explicit enough to understand easily (well, that becomes less true if you read what experts are able to do with them but that is definitely not the subject of this chapter).

An example

Let us take a simple example of a function that we can build using a combination of spreadsheet functions and then translate in Google Apps Script; I want to get the number of hours that have passed since my birthday.

Downloading the example code

You can download the example code files for all Packt books you have purchased from your account at `http://www.packtpub.com`. If you purchased this book elsewhere, you can visit `http://www.packtpub.com/support` and register to have the files e-mailed directly to you.

The spreadsheet-formula approach

A quick look at the spreadsheet function list tells us that we have a function called TODAY() that returns today's date and another one called DATE(date as a string) that returns a date in its string representation.

If we decide to subtract these two values TODAY()-DATE(1958,2,19), we obtain the number of days that have passed since my birth date until now. Let's multiply it by 24 and get the result in hours.

I was born at 2 a.m. and when I try the two functions, I get 6 p.m., so we still have to improve the formula.

Looking at the results when you run a search for the letter H, I see a function HOUR(); the documentation tells me that HOUR() returns the hour component of a specific time in the numeric format. So I try HOUR(TODAY), but this doesn't work because TODAY() has no time information; it has only the information of today's date. What about NOW()?

If I quickly try the =NOW() function in my spreadsheet; the autocomplete feature tells me that it returns the date and time information of this moment, which is exactly what I am looking for. HOUR(NOW()) returns **18**—that's correct. Since I was born at 2 a.m., let's just write HOUR(NOW())-2 to get the difference.

Now if we put it all together, we get =24*(TODAY()-DATE(1958,2,19)) +HOUR(NOW())-2, which is the formula that will return the number of hours since I was born. Great!

As you can see from the previous basic example, this is all very logical and can almost be written intuitively, following a normal human/mathematical sequence.

Now I can easily use this formula in other cells using references instead of numbers; it will adapt itself automatically and I can even use it in a table as shown in the following screenshot; dates are in column E and hours in column F and every row has a formula in column G that adapts itself automatically to match the row numbers:

D	E	F	G	H
NAME	date birth	time birth	result (hours)	
Anne	12/10/1959	12	=24*(today()-E2)+hour(now())-F2	
Lucy	3/5/1996	17	156,097	
Jordan	6/1/2001	22	110,156	
Jim	11/26/1991	8	193,570	

In the previous screenshot, you can see the formula that applies to all my family members; I just wrote it in G1 and dragged the formula down so that it is applied automatically to all the cells it was dragged over while updating its reference cells.

The previous simple example illustrates the following two elements that I wanted to focus on:

- Spreadsheet formulas are fast and relatively easy to expand when data is properly organized and we get used to their logic

- Spreadsheet formulas are rigid as they use fixed references and apply only to data that is on the document (or at least in some document/sheet, even if it is hidden)

The Google Apps Script approach – a few comments

Before we show the Google Apps Script as an equivalent, let me remind you of a couple of things.

As I mentioned before, Google spreadsheets were introduced in 2006 and had to conform to the de facto spreadsheet standard that was established by Microsoft Excel, the latter being designed in 1986 for all the spreadsheet functions but not necessarily for the included macro development.

Twenty years is a very long time in the history of computers. In 1986, few people knew about the Internet and the most popular programming languages were Fortran, Cobol, or Basic, almost all of which have now disappeared, and C was only beginning to allure a few experts.

Microsoft developed Visual Basic as the macro language behind spreadsheets. Its structure was similar to Basic, using labels, line numbers, and go tos—a structure that looks quite old fashioned to today's programmers and offers a limited development perspective.

JavaScript will have to wait another 10 years before invading our computers.

In a way, one could say it was easier for Google engineers to create the Google spreadsheet with a smarter and more powerful macro language borrowed from one of the most popular languages on the Internet behind HTML.

This little introduction is just to mention that JavaScript is probably one of the most easy-to-learn languages as far as documentation availability is concerned.

There are literally thousands of websites and blogs that offer thousands of examples, tutorials, and references about JavaScript, a lot of them being directly useable in Google Apps Script.

The Google Apps Script approach – the code

The following code illustrates the Google Apps Script approach to finding the number of hours that have passed since my birthday:

```
function myAgeInHours(){
  var myBirthDate = new Date('1958/02/19 02:00:00').getTime();
  myBirthDate = parseInt(myBirthDate/3600000, 10);
  var today = parseInt(new Date().getTime()/3600000, 10);
  return today-myBirthDate;
}
```

That's about it!

I'm joking of course, but not that much. Let's look at it more closely.

If you're reading these lines on a computer, just open your favorite browser on your favorite search engine page and type `JavaScript date` because what we are trying here concerns dates and the first line of code starts with `new Date()`.

The Internet page should now be filled with links to hundreds of pages that will explain:

Creates a JavaScript Date instance that represents a single moment in time. Date objects are based on a time value that is the number of milliseconds since 1 January, 1970 UTC.

Constructor

new Date();

new Date(value);

new Date(dateString);

new Date(year, month [, day, hour, minute, second, millisecond]);

(The preceding example is taken from: `https://developer.mozilla.org/en-US/docs/Web/JavaScript/Reference/Global_Objects/Date`.)

Having read this preceding short definition, you know everything you need to know about dates in JavaScript: it is an object (this is an important concept, so we'll come back to this later) and built using the function `new Date()`. The next three lines tell us how to give a specific value to this `Date` object, with no argument resulting in today's date and time.

The preceding definition also tells you that the value after a date is the number of milliseconds that have passed since January 1, 1970; negative values are accepted for dates prior to this reference.

Even if you hear the word JavaScript for the first time in your whole life, you cannot possibly be scared or discouraged by this, even if, as you can imagine, those will be big numbers! And indeed they are.

January 1, 2014 at 00:00 UTC is 1,388,534,400,000 milliseconds, which is a big number indeed, but that's what computers are made for — handling numbers — aren't they?

Most times, we can simply ignore this value and use its date representation instead, which reads more naturally when speaking of dates and time; but it's good to know it because we will use it to calculate the duration between two dates as we've done in our preceding example.

One of the problems that our teachers taught us to solve when we were kids was how to calculate the hours and minutes between two events knowing that there are only 60 minutes in an hour and 24 hours in a day — our first math nightmare!

Now, I have good news for you!

You can count in decimal again, JavaScript's `new Date()` method will convert dates and time formatted in decimals to the proper date and time format.

The `new Date(1388534400000)` method will return **January 1, 2014 at 00:00 UTC**; if you ever forget the reference date January 1, 1970, just type `new Date(0)` and you'll get **Thu Jan 01 01:00:00 GMT+01:00 1970** (we're even told it was a Thursday).

Let us return to our function; the very first line of this code is as follows:

```
function myAgeInHours(){
```

`function` indicates where the function starts; it's a keyword in JavaScript.

`myAgeInHours` is the name I specified for the function in this example; the rules of the language require that the name be a single word, but we'd like it to be meaningful, so we wrote this in mixed case to focus your attention on the individual words. This format is called CamelCase and is not mandatory; it's just a convention that makes code more readable.

`()` holds an optional parameter that the function will use. There can be more than one parameter (separated by commas) and they may be of any type: numbers, strings, arrays, objects, or whatever else is necessary for the function.

{ indicates the beginning of the function code; there will be a closing curly bracket at the end of our function code to indicate the end of the code. From here, we can start telling what we want the function to do, which variable to use, and what result to return.

```
var myBirthDate = new Date('1958/02/19 02:00:00').getTime();
```

This first line defines a variable (`var name = `) and gives it a name.

Note that variables in JavaScript are defined within a function and exist only within that function; in other words, you cannot use a variable value outside the scope of the function in which you defined it.

If you want a variable to be global (useable by all the functions in your script), you have to define it outside all the functions within which you want to use it and you cannot change its value from a function, that is, they will be constants!

Everything that comes after the equality sign indicates to the program what this variable is, that is, its type and value. In this case, it is a `date` object with the value February 19,1958 at 2 a.m. exactly.

Right after the `new Date()` function, we have a chained instruction using the `getTime()` method; a quick look at the page we opened in our browser will tell us that `getTime()` returns the value of the `date` object in milliseconds, which is its native value.

You may have noticed that we used a dot ( ) to chain our two instructions; that is how we can modify objects' properties (we'll learn more about this later as well).

At the end of the line is a semicolon (`;`) that indicates we are done with the line and that what is coming next is a new line of code. In Google Apps Script, the absence of this semicolon does not cause an error (it's not mandatory), but it's a good habit to use it systematically because just about every other development environment requires it and it really does improve readability. It also allows you to add a second instruction after it on the same line or add a comment that won't be interpreted if you use a double slash (`//`) before it.

```
var test = 0;// this is a variable called test and its value is 0
```

Now, we know the number of milliseconds that have passed between my birth date and January 1, 1970 at 00:00 hours and that it's a big number not really scaled to accommodate our human perception. Let us convert that into hours by dividing it by 3,600,000 (3600 seconds of 1000 milliseconds) to get only the the result in integer form.

Getting the integer from a decimal number is easy in JavaScript using one of the many methods available, such as `parseInt()` or the `Math.floor(x)` method. Some of the Internet reference sites about JavaScript show complete lists of all the available methods in each category with a few examples and basic explanations to help you choose from among them.

The following one comes from Mozilla Developer Network (`https://developer.mozilla.org/en-US/docs/Web/JavaScript/Reference/Global_Objects/parseInt`):

> *Summary*
>
> *The parseInt() function parses a string argument and returns an integer of the specified radix or base.*
>
> *Syntax*
>
> *parseInt(string, radix);*
>
> *Parameters*
>
> *string*
>
> *The value to parse. If string is not a string, then it is converted to one. Leading whitespace in the string is ignored.*
>
> *radix*
>
> *An integer that represents the radix of the above mentioned string. Always specify this parameter to eliminate reader confusion and to guarantee predictable behavior. Different implementations produce different results when a radix is not specified.*

It parses a string as an integer in decimal form when using a radix of `10`; that's what we needed.

The next lines of code are almost the same:

```
var today = parseInt(new Date().getTime()/3600000, 10);
return today-myBirthDate;
}
```

In the preceding code, `today` is a new variable that represents the number of hours since the birth date until now and `return` tells the function what value to return; in this case, it's the difference between now and my birth date, which will naturally be a positive integer.

The closing curly bracket terminates the function body as mentioned earlier.

This small code can now be saved in the script editor and doing so will force you to specify a name for this first script; just let your imagination flow freely and in the next section we will examine how to actually use it.

Using the development environment – the script editor

The script editor is a dedicated online development environment that allows for text editing, automatic code formatting, and basic error detection, it can be opened from the tools menu of a spreadsheet, the tools menu of a text document, or directly from the Google Drive home page at `https://drive.google.com` | **Create** | **Connect more apps** | **Script**. This last document type is optional in the drive interface, but once you have it activated, it will remain available. I strongly recommend that you do so if you are interested in Google Apps Script.

For now, we will use the spreadsheet interface, open the script editor from the **Tools** menu, and write the code snippet we just prepared.

The script editor is probably the best thing that has happened to me in my long journey trying to learn programming in Google Apps Script because it has a very useful feature that some people still seem to ignore: autocompletion.

The advantages of autocompletion

Autocomplete or **Content assist** (which is presently the official name of this tool) can be activated from the **Edit** menu in the script editor; the keyboard shortcut to activate it is *Ctrl* + Space bar.

This writing assistance will help you avoid a lot of errors, from simple typos to type mismatch or syntax errors because it simply suggests all the possible methods available while you are typing your code.

For example, imagine we want to get the value from the cell that is selected in the sheet with which we are working (later, we'll see in detail what this really means). The code for it is as follows:

```
1   SpreadsheetApp.getActiveSpreadsheet().getActiveSheet().getActiveCell().getValue();
```

Let's admit that this is not so simple to type in when we are new to this; using the uppercase in the right places and the importance of sequence order are not really easy to manage.

Now press *s*, just *s* and nothing else, and then hold *Ctrl* and press Space bar. The following is a screenshot of what you will see:

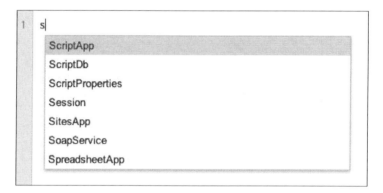

These are all the class objects available in Google Apps Script starting with letter S; you can choose the one you want with your mouse or the keyboard arrows, or even by simply adding more letters.

We want **SpreadsheetApp**, so we can select it right from the list or just type *p* and the following screenshot shows what we get:

Isn't it magic? No, there's no magic there, but it's really helpful and so easy!

This feature sometimes shows new services and methods even before they are officially announced! (Believe me, it's happened a few times that some of us discovered undocumented features just by accidentally using a keystroke.)

Anyway, even if it probably won't happen anymore since Google rewrote all its documentation recently and makes real efforts to keep it up-to-date, it is still really helpful for everybody, from an absolute beginner to a Google Apps Script expert.

As mentioned earlier, we have to use a dot to chain methods in JavaScript, so let's type a dot followed by pressing *Ctrl* + Space bar again, as shown in the following screenshot:

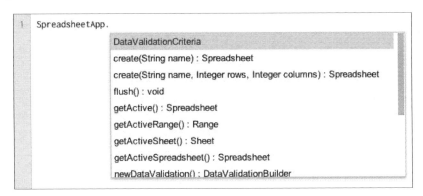

Now, the list in the previous screenshot is too long to show entirely in the small UI window, so let's narrow it down to what we are looking for, by typing the letter *g* as shown in the following screenshot:

```
1  SpreadsheetApp.g
           getActive() : Spreadsheet
           getActiveRange() : Range
           getActiveSheet() : Sheet
           getActiveSpreadsheet() : Spreadsheet
```

The choice is clear. Actually, we could use any of these methods to finally get the value in the selected cell, so let's go to the end of the process by just repeating the same workflow, as shown in the following screenshot:

```
1  SpreadsheetApp.getActiveSpreadsheet().getActiveSheet().getActiveCell().getValue();
```

I'm very happy to tell you that you just typed a beautiful line of code that is completely useless! But, at least it didn't cost you much effort.

That code is indeed not very interesting; it doesn't assign a value to a variable nor does it do anything else. It is just an example of correct syntax; correct but not useable.

The following screenshot shows a code that we could use:

```
1   var cellValue = SpreadsheetApp.getActiveSpreadsheet().getActiveSheet().getActiveCell().getValue();
```

In the single line of code shown in the previous screenshot, we create a variable (`cellValue`) and we assign it a value, which is taken from the content of the active cell. That's a good starting point.

In this example, we've assumed that the meanings of all these methods used have been clearly understood and that the choice has nothing to do with chance or hazard; that was indeed the case, but of course it won't be so clear if you have just started to work with these tools, so it might be interesting to have a quick look at it now.

Reading the documentation

The documentation on Google Apps Script is available on the Google Developers **Products** page as part of the Google Apps platform (`https://developers.google.com/apps-script/`) and shows a mix of guides, tutorials, and reference documentation along with a few links to helpful resources, including the Stack Overflow forum (`http://stackoverflow.com/questions/tagged/google-apps-script`) that I've already mentioned and where I've been participating since May 2012, which is when Google closed their Google Groups Help forum where I took my first steps in this subject. The Stack Overflow forum uses tags to sort the numerous posts; you can use this tagged link to restrict your search results to the relevant language (see *Chapter 8, How to Expand Your Knowledge*).

The very first thing we find on this web page is a search window, as illustrated in the preceding screenshot, in which we can type any keyword that we want to run a search for.

The search engine is Google's primary business, so we can be quite sure that it will return the results in a fast and reliable manner.

The results are by default restricted to Google Apps Script and suggest references to every documentation item in various categories from which you can choose. It shows a subset of its content as well.

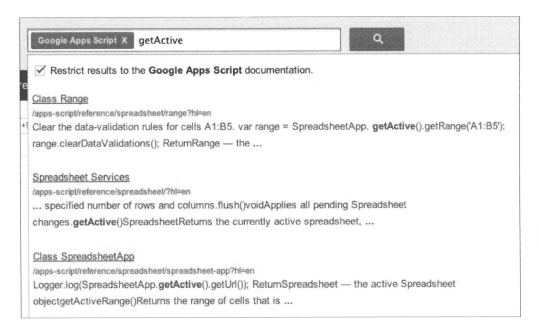

When we choose one of the search results, we arrive at the reference documentation page where we find an exhaustive list of all the available methods in the relevant category.

Most of the important methods include code examples that show you how to use them and what data they return. In many cases, the example code can be a good starting code for a beginner.

You can also look for what you need manually, of course, using the sidebar index where every Google Apps Script class opens a folder tree containing every possible method you can use.

Another option is to have a look at the quickstart and tutorials links in the **Overview** section at https://developers.google.com/apps-script/overview. I cannot recommend enough that you read this at least once, particularly if you are not familiar with program writing but also in every other case because it will show you all the possible ways to use Google Apps Script with the help of various simple examples and video presentations.

I am not going to reproduce the documentation's content in this book as that would be completely useless, so let us continue with our first step in JavaScript programming.

Earlier in this chapter, we wrote our first Google Apps Script function as follows:

```
function myAgeInHours(){
  var myBirthDate = new Date('1958/02/19 02:00:00').getTime();
  myBirthDate = parseInt(myBirthDate/3600000, 10);
  var today = parseInt(new Date().getTime()/3600000, 10);
  return today-myBirthDate;
}
```

But, we haven't really executed it yet, so let us try it now.

On top of the script editor, we have a **Run** menu and a play icon ▶ that will start executing the selected function, as shown in the following screenshot:

Clicking on the play icon or navigating to **Run | myAgeInHours** triggers the script execution; but if you try it, you will see that nothing happens. That is normal, as the function we wrote returns a result, but only in the context in which it is intended to work.

In other words, if another function would have called this function, it would have got the result as a number representing the duration in hours between now and my birth date, or if we had used the same function as a spreadsheet function, we would have seen the result in the spreadsheet cell.

Let us try this last method, better known as custom spreadsheet functions, in the next section.

Custom spreadsheet functions

We have seen how to use built-in spreadsheet functions using an equals sign before the function name; custom functions work exactly the same way.

If we type in cell **A1** the following: `=myAgeInHours()`, we will almost instantaneously get the value returned by the function, which will be something like **489,584**, and it will change every hour.

This is all very simple and quite attractive at first glance, but we'll see in the next chapter that it is not always the best way to use Google Apps Script as there are a few annoying behaviors in this workflow.

If we want to preview the result without using the spreadsheet interface, the best way to do it is using the built-in Logger or the JavaScript keyword `throw`.

The Logger result is available from the **View Logs** menu item and shows every occurrence of every `Logger.log` call that we insert in the script. In our simple example, we could write it as follows:

```
function myAgeInHours(){
  var myBirthDate = new Date('1958/02/19 02:00:00').getTime();
  Logger.log(myBirthDate);
  myBirthDate = parseInt(myBirthDate/3600000, 10);
  Logger.log(myBirthDate);
  var today = parseInt(new Date().getTime()/3600000, 10);
  Logger.log(today);
  Logger.log(today-myBirthDate);
  return today-myBirthDate;
}
```

The preceding code will return the following result in the Logger view, which is interesting but not very easy to read because it shows only numbers and we need to concentrate on the code to determine what values are exactly shown:

Logging output

[13-12-26 11:53:12:918 GMT] -3.744504E11
[13-12-26 11:53:12:919 GMT] -104014.0
[13-12-26 11:53:12:919 GMT] 385571.0
[13-12-26 11:53:12:919 GMT] 489585.0

We can easily make it more user friendly by simply adding a little information to our code. This can be achieved in two different ways: either by literally composing your result with strings and variables or using the `format` parameter in the `Logger.log` method and using the `%s` placeholder for variables (`https://developers.google.com/apps-script/reference/base/logger#log(String,Object...)`).

I'll use both methods in the following example:

```
function myAgeInHours(){
  var myBirthDate = new Date('1958/02/19 02:00:00').getTime();
  Logger.log("myBirthDate = "+myBirthDate);
  myBirthDate = parseInt(myBirthDate/3600000, 10);
  Logger.log("myBirthDate in hours (parseInt(myBirthDate/3600000, 10))
= "+myBirthDate);
  var today = parseInt(new Date().getTime()/3600000, 10);
  Logger.log("today in hours = %s",today);
  Logger.log("today-myBirthDate = %s",today-myBirthDate);
  return today-myBirthDate;
}
```

This previous code will return the following result:

Logging output

[13-12-26 12:00:03:954 GMT] myBirthDate = -374450400000
[13-12-26 12:00:03:955 GMT] myBirthDate in hours (parseInt(myBirthDate/3600000, 10)) = -104014
[13-12-26 12:00:03:955 GMT] today in hours = 385572
[13-12-26 12:00:03:955 GMT] today-myBirthDate = 489586

That is far more readable, isn't it?

Another way to get a value from a script is using the `throw` command that literally throws a message over your browser page just like any script would do, but I personally don't like it much because it shows up the same way as an error does; it makes me feel like something bad just happened.

today=385573 - myBirthDate=-104014 = 489587 (line 5, file "demo") Dismiss

Finally, since we tried this code in a spreadsheet, we have two more options to show the result:

- Using the `toast` spreadsheet method that shows a small message at the right-bottom corner of the spreadsheet for a given number of seconds without stopping execution (`https://developers.google.com/apps-script/reference/spreadsheet/spreadsheet#toast(String,String,Number)`)
- Using the so-called Browser service that works only in the context of a spreadsheet and actually shows a pop up on the spreadsheet page (`https://developers.google.com/apps-script/reference/base/browser`)

The following screenshot shows the output for the preceding example:

This last possibility is specific in that it pauses the execution of the script and waits for the user to execute some action. In the simplest case, it is just a click on the **Ok** button but we can also ask for some value using other methods from the `Browser` class, for example, we could use the following code:

```
var name = Browser.inputBox('Enter your name', Browser.Buttons.OK_
CANCEL);
```

The preceding line of code will ask the user to enter a name that will be assigned to the variable name as illustrated in the following screenshot:

Now that we are hands on with all the tools available in the script editor and know how to set and show variable names, let us try some practical examples that can make our life easier.

Formatting your spreadsheets automatically

When looking at the Spreadsheet Service documentation (`https://developers.google.com/apps-script/reference/spreadsheet/`) and particularly the `Sheet` class (`https://developers.google.com/apps-script/reference/spreadsheet/sheet`) and the `Range` class (`https://developers.google.com/apps-script/reference/spreadsheet/range`), we can see that there are a lot of available methods that allow us to modify the sheet format; in other words, we can create functions that will set up a custom page layout with a single click.

This could be very helpful when creating shared documents with people who have to fill in some data and have a bad habit of making a mess of the page layout.

For example, they might have to change the column width and sorting, background color, or even the font size and family.

It can become a real pain to check for that all the time and reset it the way you want by proceeding step-by-step in the spreadsheet user interface (this has been a live experience for me many times as I have a few, very undisciplined collaborators).

Let us wipe out the code we used so far and try the following new one:

```
function resetPageLayout() {
  var ss = SpreadsheetApp.getActiveSpreadsheet();
  var sh = ss.getSheetByName('Sheet1');
  ss.toast('Now processing your sheet','Wait a few seconds',5);
  var header1 =
sh.getRange('A1:G1').mergeAcross().setBackground('silver').
setValue('Party menu suggestion');
  var header2 =
sh.getRange(2,1,1,7).setBackground('#aaaaff').setValues([['First
Name','Last Name','Drink','Softs','Appetizers','Meal','Dessert']]);
  sh.getRange(1,1,2,7).setBorder(true,true,true,true,true,true)
    .setHorizontalAlignment('center').setVerticalAlignment('middle')
    .setFontWeight('bold').setFontSize(14);
  var columnWidth = [150,150,180,180,180,300,200];
  for(var n=0; n < columnWidth.length ; n++){
    sh.setColumnWidth(n+1,columnWidth[n]);
  }
  sh.insertColumnAfter(7).deleteColumns(8,sh.getMaxColumns()-7);
  sh.insertRows(sh.getLastRow()+1,20);
  sh.deleteRows(sh.getLastRow()+1, sh.getMaxRows()-sh.
getLastRow()-10);
  sh.getRange(3,1,sh.getMaxRows()-2,sh.getLastColumn())
    .setBorder(false, true, false, true, true,
    false);// top, left, bottom, right, vertical, horizontal
  for(var n=sh.getLastRow() ; n > 3 ; n--){
    Logger.log(n+'  '+sh.getRange(n,1,1,7).getValues())
    if(sh.getRange(n,1,1,7).getValues().toString().
replace(/,/g,'')==''){
        sh.deleteRow(n);
        Logger.log('row '+n+' deleted');
      }
    }
  }
  sh.setFrozenRows(2);
  SpreadsheetApp.flush();
  Browser.msgBox('Now your sheet should be clean again !');
}
```

Be sure you have nothing in your sheet that you would like to save as it might be deleted when this function will execute.

 If your spreadsheet settings are in a language other than English, you might need to edit the sheet name either in the script (in the third line of code) or in your spreadsheet document itself by clicking on the name at the bottom of the page.

Now you can run the code from the script editor and you will get the following pop up requesting your authorization for this script to run:

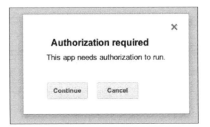

When clicking on **Continue**, you will see a second pop up with the actual authorization process along with the details of every service used by the script. In this particular case, the only service the script is using is Spreadsheet Service as we can see in the following screenshot:

Once you accept the authorization request, the script will continue to execute and you can go back to your spreadsheet to see it working live!

The following screenshot shows the formatted spreadsheet:

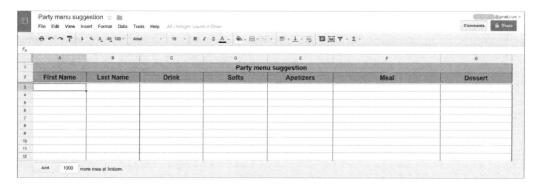

You will probably notice in the preceding screenshot that the page suggests to add 1000 rows. That is because I am using the new spreadsheet in this test. If you are still using the current standard version the number will be 20. Everything is growing with time!

At the time of writing this (December 2013), there are still a few issues with the new spreadsheet and some of the scripts described in this book are not yet available. This will be clearly highlighted when it occurs.

For up-to-date information on this, the best source is the drive support web page that is full of interesting information (https://support. google.com/drive/answer/3541068?hl=en&ref_topic=20322).

I have to admit that it takes some time to write such a script and that its use case is quite limited, but I chose this example to show a sample of the very broad panel of possibilities Google Apps Script offers and to introduce the next section in this chapter.

Menus and custom buttons in spreadsheets

Running a script from the editor might quickly become annoying as it forces us to switch between two tabs or browser windows.

That's a good opportunity to look at the menu customization and the embedded buttons.

Let's start with creating a menu by executing the following code:

```
function createMenu(){
  var menuEntries = [ {name: "resetPageLayout", functionName:"resetPa
geLayout"}];
  var sh = SpreadsheetApp.getActiveSpreadsheet();
  sh.addMenu("Format utilities",menuEntries);
}
```

 If you are using the new spreadsheet version and as described in the release note published on January 21, 2014 (https://developers.google.com/apps-script/ releases/#january_2014), a new method is available to create custom menus (the old method is still usable).

The syntax is quite different, the following code shows the new version:

```
function createMenu_new() {
  var ui = SpreadsheetApp.getUi();
  var menu = ui.createMenu ('Format utilities');
  menu.addItem ('resetPageLayout','resetPageLayout');
  menu.addToUi();
}
```

These few lines will create a custom menu in your spreadsheet as shown in the following screenshot:

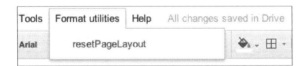

When you click on the available item, the function is called; you don't even need to open the script editor anymore.

The problem with the preceding code is that the menu will disappear when you close the document.

When you open it again, you will have to reopen the editor and run the `createMenu` function again. To get rid of that annoying task, we will use a special function named `onOpen`.

The function onOpen will execute automatically when anyone opens the spreadsheet; we'll see later that there are other such special functions that execute automatically when some event occurs.

The preceding code needs very few modifications to run automatically; just change the function name from createMenu() to onOpen().

After refreshing your browser window, you will see the new menu appear right between **Tools** and **Help**. A new bit of magic!

The other option is to include a custom button in your spreadsheet to trigger a script function you created.

From the spreadsheet menu, go to **Insert Drawing** and use the toolset to draw a button the way you like; save and close the drawing editor and your new button will be waiting for you in the spreadsheet as shown in the following screenshot:

If you click on the New button, you'll see a small menu that will allow you to assign a script function to that button as shown in the following screenshot:

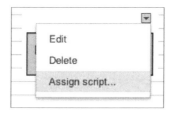

Type the name of the function you want to use as shown in the following screenshot:

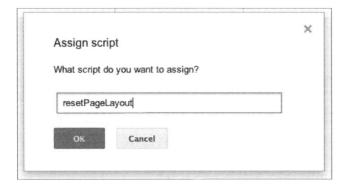

You're done! Place it where you want and enjoy.

You can use the same procedure to insert a figure that you will be able to scale to your needs and assign a function to.

 This feature (the script assignment of both drawings and figures) is not yet available in the new version of spreadsheets.

This is a pleasant feature that makes spreadsheet script comfortable to use but there are a few limitations that are listed as follows:

- The position of figures and drawings is fixed on the sheet and not on the screen; that is, when you scroll down a long list of data, the figure might disappear from the view area
- Figures and drawings cannot be inserted in the frozen rows or frozen columns area
- They can be changed, moved, or deleted by any user who has editing rights to the spreadsheet so it's not necessarily a good idea to use them in shared documents

The script from this example is probably a bad example of button or custom menu use, as both will be available to every user who can edit the document; your friends might be surprised by its effects but this was, of course, just an example.

We'll see in the next part that this example script is not ideally written as far as speed and efficiency are concerned.

Reading and writing data from spreadsheets – best practices and performances

You probably noticed when playing with the preceding script example that it takes some time to execute. You must remember how these spreadsheets and scripts actually work.

The sheet we see in our browser does not exist as a file in our computer; all its data is stored on a Google server somewhere and it is rendered as HTML content that can be understood by any web browser.

Each time we make a change manually or using a script, the information is sent to the server, interpreted, processed, and sent back to us using our Internet connection.

This can be a time-consuming journey for all those bytes; some parameters are predictable (our average connection speed, for example) and some are not, such as the distance from our computer to the Google server and its load at that moment. Remember that you are not alone in using this drive app! There can be thousands of users sending requests simultaneously.

To make things better, or at least the best we can achieve with the parameters we have control over, we should take care to use as few separate requests as possible to any distant service.

For example, if we want to fill 100 cells in a sheet column, it would be a bad idea to fill each cell one by one. We should try to use the `batch` method to set the values in all 100 cells in one single step.

Example

The following are two scripts that do what we suggested in the preceding section: filling a column of 100 cells with some text. Try both versions successively and compare the execution times of both versions, which will be shown in a browser pop up. The following code snippet fills a column of 100 cells with some text:

```
function fill100Cells(){
  var start = new Date().getTime();
  var sh = SpreadsheetApp.getActiveSpreadsheet().getActiveSheet();
  for(var n=1 ; n<=100 ;n++){
```

```
      sh.getRange(n,1).setValue('This cell is filled');
  }
  Browser.msgBox('Execution time : '+(new Date().getTime()-start)+'
milliseconds');
}

function fill100CellsatOnce(){
  var start = new Date().getTime();
  var sh = SpreadsheetApp.getActiveSpreadsheet().getActiveSheet();
  sh.getRange(1,1,100,1).setValue('This cell is filled');
  Browser.msgBox('Execution time :
    '+(new Date().getTime()-start)+' milliseconds');
}
```

The following screenshot displays the execution time for filling a column of 100 cells with some text:

I'll let you guess which one is the most efficient.

This simple example illustrates the very few annoying aspects of cloud computing and Google Drive applications, in particular, the execution speed of code.

Knowing that, we should always be very careful when writing scripts, do it as efficiently as possible, and using as few service calls as possible. These recommendations and a few others that we shall examine later on are clearly explained in Google Drive's documentation. I suggest you read it twice rather than once and keep it in mind when writing your future applications (https://developers.google.com/apps-script/best_practices).

There have been a couple of very interesting posts on that subject on the Stack Overflow Help forum and I suggest that you read this as well, as it goes quite deeper in the speed testing and optimization process (among others: http://stackoverflow.com/questions/15145918/what-is-faster-scriptdb-or-spreadsheetapp/15149959#15149959).

Catching events

An event is when something happens. That's a rather basic definition but it gives a pretty exact idea of what it means in the context of a Google spreadsheet document.

If a user modifies a cell, deletes a row or column, or even just opens a spreadsheet, all of these events can be caught by a script and we, as script writers, can decide to use these triggers to execute some task.

The online documentation (`https://developers.google.com/apps-script/understanding_events`) provides an exhaustive list of all the event sources and how to get information from them; I won't reproduce all the descriptions here but I'd like to present some interesting, useful perspectives.

Application examples are numerous: we could interact with range values, colors, font sizes or weights, and even use services that are not actually related to spreadsheets, such as modifying another document, a website's content, or sending an e-mail.

We'll see in *Chapter 4*, *Embedding Scripts in Text Documents* that the different Google services can interact very easily and manage some complex workflows automatically, but for now let us concentrate on the basic spreadsheet-related triggers and events (`https://developers.google.com/apps-script/understanding_triggers#ActionTriggers`).

There are basically two categories of triggers: simple triggers and installable triggers.

The major differences between these triggers are about authority and permissions, so the real question is which trigger is doing what?

Who is doing what? Script authorizations

As presented in Google's documentation, on one side, we have the user at the keyboard and on the other side, the script's author who installed the trigger; that is one aspect of the question and the other is the type of trigger: simple or installable.

Simple triggers run as the user at the keyboard, whether they are anonymous or logged in as an authorized editor, and therefore, simple triggers can only perform actions that don't require specific authorization or to connect to any service that needs authentication.

Following the same logic and knowing that triggers respond to events without informing the user, that is, silently, any installable trigger created by the script author will always run as if the author was running it, that is, under the authority of the author who installed the trigger.

That logic is very simple and easy to understand, but it's important to remember that when setting up a script that uses triggers.

We have seen before that some scripts require authorization before they actually execute; this is the case when a script is able to modify something or perform some action under the user's authority. For example, if you use a script to send an e-mail from your account, you would expect the script to warn you before doing it, right?

So it does; every reference or call to a nonanonymous service in a script file is analyzed when we try to run any function in that script or try to save a trigger for that script (by navigating to **Resources | Current project's trigger | Add a new one** in the menu bar) and ask for explicit authorization before its execution.

If you are not the owner of the script and you try to execute such a function, you will also be asked for explicit authorization, receive an e-mail that confirms that you have granted this script access to your data, and get a link that you can use to revoke the authorization.

This might seem like a complex procedure, but it's really a major security and privacy aspect that Google took care of, to handle in a secure manner.

Protecting your data

While we are taking care of data privacy, let's have a quick peek at data protection using Google Apps Script.

Google has introduced this ability quite recently and it opens a few interesting perspectives.

The following is an example of a script that protects a sheet after a user has added a value in a particular cell:

```
function myFunction(e) {
  var sheetIndex = e.source.getSheets().length;// to know how many
sheets we already have
  var sourceValues =
    e.source.getActiveSheet().getDataRange().getValues();//
    get all the data from this sheet
```

```
var cell = e.source.getActiveRange().getA1Notation();//
    get A1 notation for comfort of use
Logger.log('SheetName:'+e.source.getActiveSheet().getSheetName()
    +' user:'+Session.getActiveUser());
if(cell=='A1' && e.source.getSheetName()=='Sheet1'){
    // execute only if cell A1 and Sheet1, else do nothing
  var copy =
    e.source.insertSheet('SheetCopy_'+sheetIndex,sheetIndex);//
        create a copy at the last index
  copy.getRange(1,1,sourceValues.length,sourceValues[0]
    .length).setValues(sourceValues);//
      clone sheet1 values only, no format
  var permissions = copy.getSheetProtection();
  permissions.removeUser(Session.getActiveUser());//
      who is editing ? remove him from editors (does not work for
owner of course)
  permissions.setProtected(true);
  copy.setSheetProtection(permissions);//
      protect the copy, the original editor of the sheet can't change
it anymore
  e.source.getSheetByName('Sheet1').activate();//
      reset the browser to Sheet 1, not on the copy
  }
}
```

The previous code is pretty funny as it will make a copy of the active sheet on certain conditions and prevent even the user from modify it. One could imagine following such a process as signing a document and preventing its modification thereafter.

It shows that any workflow can be automated quite easily.

Also note that this code does not work with new spreadsheets for now (as of January 2014, the new version of spreadsheet (which is an optional update) doesn't support the onEdit trigger, so this function can't be implemented) and must be tested on a shared document; the actual user must NOT be the owner of the document, but an editor (perhaps with shared edit permissions).

It is indeed not possible to restrict the sheet access for the sheet owner themselves (and that's a good thing!).

Publishing your data on the Web

Spreadsheets can be published on a website (`https://support.google.com/drive/answer/37579?hl=en`) but cannot be edited from within a web page:

For this reason, there is no way to execute script functions from a web-published spreadsheet. There is very little chance that this would ever happen because of the obvious security issue it would represent.

Printing and exporting the result

As of this writing (December 2013), Google Apps Script has no possible way to print a document. Printing all or part of a spreadsheet is a common activity, one that we might want to automate using a script. Unfortunately, security considerations limit Google Apps Script access to local resources such as printers.

As a workaround for this limitation, our script can export spreadsheets to PDF and send them by e-mail or store them in Google Drive.

A quick example that won't need too much explanation is as follows:

```
function sendThisSsAsPdf(){
  var ss = SpreadsheetApp.getActiveSpreadsheet();
  var ssID = ss.getId();// get the file unique id to use with driveApp
  var pdf = DriveApp.getFileById(ssID).getAs('application/pdf');//
    get the file content in PDF format
  var saveCopy = DriveApp.createFile(pdf);//
    create a copy in your drive
  MailApp.sendEmail(Session.getEffectiveUser().getEmail(),
    'This is a copy of your spreadsheet','This is a pdf copy
    of your spreadsheet as an attachment to this message\n'+
```

```
                        'This mail was sent to you on
      '+Utilities.formatDate(new Date(), Session.getTimeZone(),
      "MMM-dd-yyyy @ HH:mm"),{attachments : [pdf]});//
      send the email with a simple message
  }
```

The preceding script shows how to simply and rapidly create a PDF version of the current spreadsheet and send it to the user at the keyboard; this function can be called from a menu of course, but can also be sent at a fixed time every single day if you need an archive copy for any reason.

In the next chapter, we'll see how to create and use Google forms as they are probably the second most-frequent entry point to Google Apps Script for most new users.

Summary

This long chapter about Google Apps Script in spreadsheets has shown that many aspects of a spreadsheet document could be modified using Google Apps Script; not only the layout and format, but the sharing and publishing features as well. What we'll learn in the coming chapters is how we can use it to exchange data with other Google services, either as a recipient or as a data source. The first example of this interaction is probably the most common: Google forms.

2

Create and Manipulate Forms

In January 2013, Google launched a new version of Google forms that was more customizable, richer in many new features, shareable between any number of editors, and—even more important to us—could be created and modified using Google Apps Script.

This feature made it possible to imagine a lot of potential applications. Some of these applications could be used for the following:

- To change questions every day, automatically
- To modify the form for future respondents based on responses from the past
- To remove or add questions depending on any external parameter (such as the day of the week or the time of day)

What tools do we have?

The forms service has quite a lot of methods presented in the Google documentation, but some of the aspects of form creation and modification are still a bit complex to apprehend (`https://developers.google.com/apps-script/reference/forms/`).

To create a form, we only need a script in a project. This project can either be bound to a document or can be a standalone file in your drive.

Since the script actually creates a new form and a new spreadsheet to get responses from, we have no special interest in using a spreadsheet-bounded script or a form-bounded one. The following code creates a simple form; its contents are directly inspired by the example that Google provides in its documentation. We will see what we can do with it using only script. It will be an opportunity to see how we can change the form content and presentation (read the comments if you're not sure how it works).

```
// Global variable = constants
var ssId = ScriptProperties.getProperty('ssId');
if(ssId == null){
```

```
  // test if the destination spreadsheet already exists, if not just
create it
  var ss = SpreadsheetApp.create('Form response spreadsheet');
  ssId = ss.getId();
  ScriptProperties.setProperty('ssId',ssId);
}


function createForm(){
  var formID = ScriptProperties.getProperty('formId');
  if(formID != null){
    // if the form was already created then do nothing
    throw('Form already exists') ; return ;
  }
  // here we create the form with questions and set the destination
spreadsheet
  var form = FormApp.create('New custom Form for test');
  form.addTextItem().setTitle('What is your last name ?').
setHelpText('Please don\'t be shy...');
  form.setDestination(FormApp.DestinationType.SPREADSHEET, ssId);
  var item = form.addCheckboxItem();
  item.setTitle('What are you ?');
  item.setChoices([
    item.createChoice('A man'),
    item.createChoice('A boy'),
    item.createChoice('A woman'),
    item.createChoice('A girl')
  ]);
  form.addMultipleChoiceItem().setHelpText('If this question bothers
you then just skip it')
  .setTitle('Do you prefer cars or dolls?')
  .setChoiceValues(['Cars','Dolls'])
  .showOtherOption(true)
  form.addDateItem()
  .setTitle('When were you born?');
  form.addGridItem()
  .setTitle('Rate your interests')
  .setRows(['Cars', 'Dolls', 'Food'])
  .setColumns(['annoying', 'no opinion', 'exciting']);
  ScriptProperties.setProperty('formId',form.getId());
  ss.getSheets()[0].getRange(1,1,4,2).setValues([['form Url',form.
getPublishedUrl()],
    ['form Edit Url',form.getEditUrl()],['formID',formID],['Spreadsheet
Url',ss.getUrl()]]);
  ss.getSheets()[0].setColumnWidth(1,200).setColumnWidth(2,800);
```

```
Logger.log('\n\nForm Url = '+form.getEditUrl()+'\n\nGoto this url and
paste the code in the FORM script editor\n'+
            '(only code from the 2cond script file : "Form Code to
copy")\n\nThen you won\'t need this script anymore\n\Thank you :-)');
}
```

When you run the preceding code from the script editor, and after granting the necessary authorizations, nothing seems to happen because all it does is create a new form and spreadsheet that will appear in your drive. Please take the time to read the logger's content after you run the code as it will give you a word of explanation. A sample of this content is shown in the following screenshot:

Logging output

[13-12-28 15:06:27:223 CET]

Form Url =
https://docs.google.com/forms/d/1Py0Uzt9ytpHTA7OtmvM263ZoOfWaODBRYvnW4SL0WIs/edit

Goto this url and paste the code in the FORM script editor
(only code from the 2cond script file : "Form Code to copy")

Then you won't need this script anymore
Thank you :-)

You can then have a look at the instructions to copy and paste some code in the newly created form script editor.

Before we get to that part though, let's have a look at how the preceding script works.

```
var ssId = ScriptProperties.getProperty('ssId');
if(ssId == null){ // test if the destination spreadsheet already
exists
  // if not just create it
  var ss = SpreadsheetApp.create('Form response spreadsheet');
  ssId = ss.getId();
  ScriptProperties.setProperty('ssId',ssId);
```

ScriptProperties is a special class that offers an easy way to store any information within the script file itself. Data stored in this form is visible to anyone who has access to the script.

Data is stored as string key / string value pairs and must have a limited size (9 KB / value = 9000 digits and 500 KB / total properties in a script). When a pair of data has not been defined yet, the method getProperty('key') returns null (meaning not defined).

We use this method to determine if the spreadsheet has already been created. We also use the exact same procedure later to know if the form has been created. This gives us a convenient method to store the form and spreadsheet IDs.

If ever we would like to create a new form/spreadsheet again, a simple function that clears the `ScriptProperties` class would reset the process and restart as new. Here is how it goes:

```
function resetAllKeys(){
 var keys = ScriptProperties.getKeys();// get every keys in this
script
 for(var n in keys){ScriptProperties.deleteProperty(keys[n])};// and
delete them one by one
}
```

We will see later in this book that `scriptProperties` and the per user equivalent `UserProperties` are real lifesavers in many situations where we have to store some values permanently. Small pieces of code such as the preceding one demonstrate how simple it is to get it working.

The main part of the code simply creates a few questions of different types. Honestly, we could easily use the "normal" form creation interface; it would surely be easier since we would be able to see what we do. The pleasure of WYSIWYG interfaces!

But this book is all about the creation of forms with Apps Script, so let's do this the hard way!

The last portion of the code adds a few important snippets of information to our newly created spreadsheet, which we'd like to have at hand for future use, and shows a message in the logger in case we forget how this script is supposed to be used in a couple of months.

Now that the form exists, we can check if everything looks like we want it to look. If not, we can always adjust it using the edit form URL. There is no need to return to our code and restart from scratch.

The next part will be more fun as we shall try to analyze the form's content and modify it a bit depending on the responses we get.

The idea is to show for each question what the last person's answer was who filled the form and who they were. In the process, we shall try out some user interface elements that will be detailed in *Chapter 7, Using User Interfaces in Spreadsheets and Documents*.

When we ran the form creation code previously, it created a spreadsheet and a form as well. The following code should be pasted in the form's script editor because its purpose is to extend the form editor user interface (for this, we need to navigate to **Tools | Script editor**).

I've added a lot of comments in the code to explain how it works and split it across separate functions.

The onOpen function simply creates the first sidebar that will suggest that we call the menu function. It creates the menu as well, as follows:

```
function onOpen() {
  var ui = FormApp.getUi();
  ui.createMenu('Form Custom Tools')
  .addItem("Show answers in questions", 'showAnswers')
  .addToUi();
  // this is how we add a menu in this type of doc, it is slightly
different from what we used in spreadsheets
  showTempSideBar();
}
```

The following function creates a simple message that asks our user to use the menu:

```
function showTempSideBar() {
  // this shows a temporary sidebar in the main user interface
  // it will be explained in detail in chapter 7
  var ui = FormApp.getUi();
  app = UiApp.createApplication().setTitle("Custom Tools User
Interface").setWidth(300)
  .setTitle("Information sidebar used as a logger").setWidth(300);
  var message = app.createHTML("If you open this page for the first
time<br>"+
    "please authorize using any item from<br>the menu : <b>'Form
Custom Tools'</b><br>"+
    "<p>This sidebar will show you some<br>informations when you run
<br>a function from the menu...")
    .setStyleAttribute('padding','20px').setId('message');
  ui.showSidebar(app.add(message));
}
```

The showAnswers() function is the main function called from the menu. In turn, it calls all the other functions to create the main sidebar and update its values. It also sends an e-mail with a summary of answers (we'll see how to send mails in more detail in the next chapter). Refer to the following code:

```
function showAnswers(){
  var app = UiApp.createApplication().setTitle("Custom Tools User
Interface").setWidth(300);
```

```
app.add(app.createHTML('These are the last values<br>entered in the
form').setStyleAttributes({'padding':'20px','background':'brown','colo
r':'beige'}));
// set some style on this Ui to get a nice look then align items in
a grid
var panel = app.createVerticalPanel().setId('panel').setStyleAttribu
tes({'fontSize':'12pt','background':'beige','color':'#333333','padding
':'10px'}).setHeight('100%').setWidth('100%');
var grid = app.createGrid(12,2).setText(0,1,'Questions overview').
setText(6,1,'Responses');
// don't forget to add the panel to the Ui and the grid to the panel
app.add(panel.add(grid));
var form = FormApp.getActiveForm();//access this form
var sh = SpreadsheetApp.openById(form.getDestinationId()).
getSheetByName('Form Responses');
//read the whole spreadsheet and get values in an array
var data = sh.getDataRange().getValues();
var lc = sh.getLastColumn();
// we have seen how to clean up a sheet, let's remove unnecessary
columns and set appropriate width
sh.insertColumnAfter(lc).deleteColumns(lc+1,sh.getMaxColumns()-lc);
sh.setColumnWidth(1,160);
// last row of data (=last item in the array)is last answer
var lastResponse = data.pop();
var lastUser = lastResponse[1];
// second field is the lastName item (arrays count from 0), shift
the array row to get rid of timeStamp in column1
lastResponse.shift();
var questions = form.getItems();
// get all questions and iterate these questions array using the
Logger to check content
var textToSend = 'Summary of last form response\n';
for(var n in questions){
  Logger.log(questions[n].getTitle()+' = '+questions[n].getIndex());
  // for the 3 first question there is only 1 answer
  var response = lastResponse[n];
  // if response is a date, transform it to a user-friendly
formatted string
  if(typeof(response)=='object'){response = Utilities.
formatDate(response,Session.getTimeZone(),'yyyy/MM/dd')};
  // the 4th question has 3 choices, show all of them joined
together with '&'
  if(n>3){response = lastResponse.splice(4,3).join(' & ')};
  // and update the question help value
```

```
      questions[n].setHelpText(lastUser+' has answered "'+response+'",
  what would you answer ?');
      updateUi(app,grid,n,questions,response);
      textToSend += '\n'+questions[n].getTitle()+'\t'+response
  }
    MailApp.sendEmail(Session.getActiveUser().getEmail(),'Summary of
  last form response',textToSend);
    var ui = FormApp.getUi();
    ui.showSidebar(app);
  }
```

The following function uses five parameters (the names are mentioned in parenthesis); some are related to the user interface and others are values. Note the simplicity of this mechanism: any parameter we need can simply be added to any function.

```
  function updateUi(app,grid,n,questions,response){
    app = showData(grid,n,0,n+' : ' );// display question number
    app = showData(grid,n,1,questions[n].getTitle());// display question
  title
    app = showData(grid,Number(n)+6,0,n+' : ');// display response
  number
    app = showData(grid,Number(n)+6,1,response);//display response value
  }
```

What follows is probably the shortest function in this book. I have used it mainly for demonstration purposes; it could easily be integrated into another function.

```
  function showData(grid,row,col,text){
    grid.setText(Number(row)+1,col,text);
  }
```

Once everything is copied in place and saved, you can refresh your browser window to let the onOpen function get executed; you should see a new sidebar on the right of your screen along with some explanation.

Before running any function, you should fill a form so you have at least one row of data to play with. But if you don't, it's not really an issue. The link to the form is available in the menu as shown in the following screenshot:

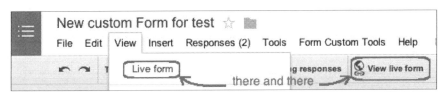

Now follow the instructions, run a function from the custom menu, and look at the result. We wanted the form to show the last answer, and so it does!

It certainly isn't the most useful script in history, but it shows how we can interact with forms using script. It also gave us the opportunity to get a quick peek at the HTML and UiApp services that will allow us to go further in our customization.

Forms' limitations

There are a few things we cannot achieve with `FormApp`. For example, there is no way to catch user response and modify a form according to their answers. The only form-related event that we can catch is the form submission itself; that is, we can catch the occurrence of an event when the form is submitted and all the data is already recorded. It's a major limitation of this service, but we'll see that it's possible to do so using other approaches.

Handling answers

The function we wrote in the script earlier will not be very useful if we have to run it manually (we won't be there to monitor every time someone fills a form). So, we should capture the event when someone sends a form so that we are informed by an e-mail message.

We already see the events available in the spreadsheet, so we know how it works. Just go to the **Resources** menu in the script editor to set up a new trigger **On form submit** as shown in the following screenshot:

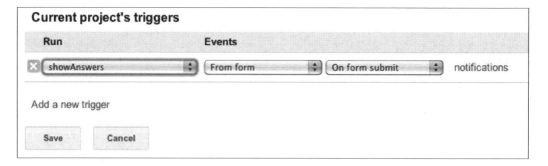

Now the script will send us a message every time a form is filled. Note that the sidebar UI won't be updated since it can only work in cases where a user actually uses the form editor UI.

Forms' alternatives

If you need to customize your forms further than what Google's forms service offers or if you don't like to see Google's messages and logo on all the forms you send (these are indeed quite obvious), Google Apps Script has two UI-oriented services you can use. Both are capable of developing very complex UIs, the second being even more powerful as it includes the possibility to use external JavaScript libraries, such as jQuery.

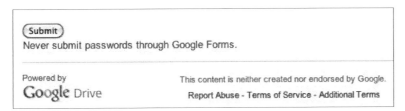

A quick peek at the UiApp and HTML services

We saw in the previous form example that we can create small user interfaces to enhance the standard form UI. This is also available in documents and spreadsheets, although it is slightly different. I decided to use both of them in this small example to encourage you to experiment and customize more because, even if it takes some time to develop these tools, it is so rewarding from a personal point of view that it's well worth the pain.

UiApp was the first service available in Google Apps Script a few years ago and is still presented as experimental in the documentation, although no announcement has been made (for now) that they will deprecate it in the near future. Google encourages users to switch to an HTML service as this one will continue to be upgraded.

In the meantime, we will continue to show both of them as they both have strengths and weaknesses.

Summary

A forms service can actually be very useful to teachers or other people who need to create lots of forms or questionnaires, often using the same structure.

The ability forms have to respond to triggers provides the possibility to automatically send back an evaluation with reference to good and bad answers.

The academic community is probably the group most interested in this Google app.

It gives us the opportunity to use function parameters to split our code into smaller and simpler parts.

Our last example introduced the key word of the next chapter: e-mail.

Managing an E-mail Account

3

One of the reasons I began using Google Drive and Google Apps Script is that I had a Gmail account for my personal mail service, and the school I work for decided to get Google Apps for educational accounts in 2009.

This choice was probably made because not only did it seem complete and efficient, but also because it was free.

If you are interested in Google Apps Script, you are most probably a Gmail user too, so this chapter might interest you a lot.

The Gmail Browser UI has a lot of built-in tools that work pretty well; you can search, sort, archive, and delete about everything you want in a couple of clicks; you can create filters, labels, and automatically forward mails very easily too; and to be honest with you, you won't be able to do a lot more with Google Apps Script!

Bad news?

Not sure. However, there are two things that you will be able to control: how and when to use the built-in tools offered by the Google Apps Script.

Let's take a simple example; you want to set up a filter that sets a label on every message coming from your boss. However, you also want to keep an archive of it in a document along with a link to the attachments stored in your drive to be able to quickly search any reference he might have sent you. You would prefer that his e-mail messages remain in your main mailbox for the whole day to be sure that you don't forget to read them.

How would you achieve this workflow in Gmail? Could you do it in your mail-client application/program? Not sure of either? Well, a script can do this quite easily and we will take that use case as a practical example.

We need the following:

- A way to know who the sender of the mail is (`https://developers.google.com/apps-script/reference/gmail/gmail-message#getFrom()`)

- A way to get the message content as text (`https://developers.google.com/apps-script/reference/gmail/gmail-message#getPlainBody()`)

- A place to store that text (`https://developers.google.com/apps-script/reference/document/document-app#create(String)`)

- A way to get the attachments and store them in a drive folder (`https://developers.google.com/apps-script/reference/gmail/gmail-message#getAttachments()`)

- A link to each of these files at hand near the message (`https://developers.google.com/apps-script/reference/drive/file#getUrl()`)

- A tool to set labels (`https://developers.google.com/apps-script/reference/gmail/gmail-thread#addLabel(GmailLabel)`)

- A tool to create a label when it's missing (`https://developers.google.com/apps-script/reference/gmail/gmail-app#createLabel(String)`)

- A timer or a clock to filter the messages at night when you sleep, so they are clearly visible during your working day (`https://developers.google.com/apps-script/understanding_triggers#TimeTriggers`)

Note that all the links in the preceding list take you to the relevant services and methods that we shall use; you may want to read it beforehand or keep reading and get to it later on. But, in any case, I'd recommend that you take the time to read it thoroughly so that everything becomes clear and looks logical to you. Understanding exactly what we do is, in my humble opinion, the only way to learn something and remember it (just saying that I'm certainly not innovating).

I could have presented a piece of code that does all this in one go and tried to explain it step-by-step, but I'm afraid that it would have become confusing and, most of all, I'm not sure if this workflow will be useful for anyone as it is. So, let's try and solve each piece of the puzzle separately and assemble them at the end of this chapter to get a fully-working demo.

Retrieving Gmail data

After a couple of years, a normal user's Gmail account is often a compilation of thousands of threads and a lot more messages of all kinds. Some have labels, some remain unread sometimes; I even know people who never delete or archive anything and it can easily become a real mess.

Let us assume you are not one of these people and that you already have a couple of labels to sort your messages in a clever way.

The Gmail app is a service that provides methods to retrieve messages in many ways. We can get all threads without any criteria, threads with a specific label, starred threads, and a few other threads but in this first example, we will focus on our inbox threads (`https://developers.google.com/apps-script/reference/gmail/gmail-app#getInboxThreads()`).

If you look at the documentation, you'll find two occurrences of the `getInboxThreads()` method; one has no parameter and the other has two parameters—start and max—to retrieve partial data so that we can process them in small batches.

The reason for this is that it takes some time to retrieve data from Gmail and if we have a lot of messages, it could easily take too long.

 I haven't yet mentioned a very important aspect of Google Apps Script: the execution time of any script is limited to about five minutes, no matter what you are trying to do or which Google account you have. After five minutes, the execution will stop and you will get a message: **Exceeded maximum execution time**.

Knowing this constraint, we will limit our script to as few threads as possible for now, so we don't exceed any limit. The `getInboxThreads(start, max)` method with parameters will be helpful.

A bit later, when we need to process a lot of data, we'll discover how to handle this situation (see the *Execution time versus time limit* section).

Once we have a thread object (`https://developers.google.com/apps-script/reference/gmail/gmail-thread`), we can apply a method to get a message object (`https://developers.google.com/apps-script/reference/gmail/gmail-message`). Remember that JavaScript is an object-oriented language; each object has properties, and the autocomplete feature (and the documentation also, of course) will show us all the available methods to get these properties.

We want to get the message's sender, text, and the attachments. The following code shows you how it works in a function that gets the most recent message to your inbox and sends you back its content as a PDF file for the body, along with a copy of the attachment in its original format:

```
function getAttachAndBody(){
  var firstThread = GmailApp.getInboxThreads(0,1)[0];
```

```
    // get only the most recent thread
    var message = firstThread.getMessages()[0];
    // get the first message in that thread,getMessages() returns an
array of message objects
    var sender = message.getFrom();
    // get the sender email
    var attach = message.getAttachments();
    // get the attachment
    var body = message.getBody();
    //body as a string
    var bodyDocHtml = DocsList.createFile('body.html', body, "text/
html");
    // create a html file with the body content
    var bodyId=bodyDocHtml.getId();// get its id
    var bodyDocPdf = bodyDocHtml.getAs('application/pdf').getBytes();
    // convert this html in pdf
    var bodyToSend = {fileName: 'body.pdf',content:bodyDocPdf,
      mimeType:'application/pdf'};
    // bodyToSend is the object containing the pdf
    if(attach.length>0){
      // if attachment in original message send it along with the msg
body to the current user.
      MailApp.sendEmail(Session.getEffectiveUser().getEmail(),
        'transfer email text received from '+sender+' as pdf + body &
attachment in attachment', 'see attachments',
                        {attachments:[attach[0],bodyToSend]});
      }
    MailApp.sendEmail(Session.getEffectiveUser().getEmail(),
      'transfer email text received from '+sender+' as pdf in
        attachment', 'see attachments', {attachments:[bodyToSend]});
    // if no attachment just send the pdf version of message text
    DocsList.getFileById(bodyId).setTrashed(true);
    // delete the html message from your drive as it was a temporary
item we don't need anymore.
    }
```

In this simple example, we intentionally neglected a few parameters to keep it as simple as possible; we considered only the first message of the first thread and assumed that there was only one attached file in this message. We'll see later how to develop the script, so as to be more close to real situations.

We also made use of a service we haven't mention yet, DocsList, which is still marked as experimental and is probably going to be replaced by the more recent Drive service, which offers similar methods but uses another approach in some aspects. This will be examined in the next chapter.

Now, let us focus on one of the most useful Gmail features—labels.

Creating labels

Labels in Gmail can be considered as an equivalent to folders; they allow us to sort messages in as many categories as we want, to make them easier to find when we need to.

There is already, by default, a spam filter in your Gmail account and a newly introduced feature that shows promotions, social networks, and forum threads separately, but we might want to be more selective and have separate labels for all our mail activities.

As far as I am concerned, I like that every thread has a label. My computer (and its related online data) is the only thing that I keep tidy; too bad that's not the the case with my desktop.

So, I created labels for every possible type of e-mails: Facebook, Stack Overflow forum, computer spare parts distributors, audio equipment ads, and so on.

I might have done that using Gmail filters of course, or using my favorite mail-client application, but I did it with Google Apps Script; go figure out why.

Creating a label is very straightforward, as shown in the documentation (https://developers.google.com/apps-script/reference/gmail/gmail-app#createLabel(String)):

```
GmailApp.createLabel('Label Name');
```

If we want to check whether a label already exists before creating it, we can write a more sophisticated function as follows (along with a function to test it):

```
function createLabel(labelName){
  if( ! GmailApp.getUserLabelByName(labelName)){
    GmailApp.createLabel(labelName);
  }
  var info = 'Label "'+labelName+'" now exists and has '+GmailApp.
getUserLabelByName(labelName).getThreads().length
  +' threads, '+GmailApp.getUserLabelByName(labelName).
getUnreadCount()+' unread threads' ;// prepare a readable message
  return info
}

function testLabelNameCreation(){
 Logger.log(createLabel('testLabelTodelete'));// open the logger to
read the message
}
```

This is all very simple and it wouldn't be too hard for you to adapt it to your needs. If you expect to create a lot of labels, use the preceding code in a loop and define your label names in an array of strings:

```
function createManyLabels(){
  var labels = ['test1','test2','test3','test4'];
  for(var n in labels){
    Logger.log(createLabel(labels[n]));
  }
}
```

Be careful when you use this script because it can take some time to execute; the preceding example with four labels took 15 seconds to run, so don't try to create hundreds of labels at once!

If you have tried this code and want to delete the test labels, you can use the `delete` method of the `GmailLabel` class, I'll let you find how to change the preceding code to delete the labels it created (`https://developers.google.com/apps-script/reference/gmail/gmail-label#deleteLabel()`).

Counting, sorting, archiving, and deleting e-mails and threads

We have seen in the earlier examples that it is quite easy to manipulate threads and messages with regard to labels.

Once we get a thread object, we can do what we want with it. A quick look at the documentation shows the many methods available but as I have already mentioned, these operations might take some time and we may easily face issues with the maximum execution time limit of five minutes.

Execution time versus time limit

The solution to this is to proceed with relatively small bunches of threads. A careful approach is to treat 100 threads at a time and continue as long as we need or until it is finished.

Google Apps Script has all the tools we need:

- A programmable time trigger to automate the process
- A convenient place to store the number of processed items
- A way to delete the trigger when it is finished

The following code is an example that will examine all your e-mails and add labels inside every thread according to the thread's original label; it will send you an e-mail with a logger view of its activity (an activity report) and the current progress of the task and stop automatically when everything is done. Then, you'll receive a last mail to warn you that everything is over.

The script is fairly long but it has (hopefully) enough comments in every step to help you understand how it works. It will of course ask for a few authorizations: Gmail, Script Properties, and session identity:

```
function inboxLabeller() {
    // check if the script runs for the first time or not,
    // if so, create the trigger and ScriptProperties the script will
use
    // a start index and a total counter for processed items
    // else continue the task
    if(ScriptProperties.getKeys().length==0){
        ScriptProperties.setProperties({'threadStart':0,
'itemsprocessed':0, 'notFinished':true});
        ScriptApp.newTrigger('inboxLabeller').timeBased().
everyMinutes(10).create();
    }
    // initialize all variables when we start a new task, "notFinished"
is the main loop condition
    var items = Number(ScriptProperties.getProperty('itemsprocessed'));
    var tStart = Number(ScriptProperties.getProperty('threadStart'));
    var notFinishedinished = ScriptProperties.getProperty('notFinished'
)=='true';
    Logger.clear();// be sure the Logger is empty

    while (notFinishedinished){ // the main loop
        var threads = GmailApp.getInboxThreads(tStart,100);
        getAds(tStart);// check if it's an ad and move it to "Ads" folder
if necessary
        Logger.log('Number of threads='+Number(tStart+threads.length));
        if(threads.length==0){ // if no threads anymore the we're done
            notFinishedinished=false; // reset the flag
            break;//and exit the loop
        }
        for(t=0;t<threads.length;++t){
            var mCount = threads[t].getMessageCount();// how many messages ?
            var mSubject = threads[t].getFirstMessageSubject();
            var labels = threads[t].getLabels();
            var labelsNames = '';
```

```
      for(var l in labels){labelsNames+=labels[l].getName()};
      // get all the labels even if more than one for each message and
write this in the logger
      Logger.log('subject '+mSubject+' has '+mCount+' msgs with labels
'+labelsNames);
      for(var l in labels){
        // assign the label to every message in the thread
        labels[l].addToThread(threads[t]);
      }
    }
  }
    tStart = tStart+100;// prepare for next execution
    items = items+100;// to start from the next bunch
    ScriptProperties.setProperties({'threadStart':tStart,
'itemsprocessed':items});// store this value
    break;
  }
  if(notFinishedinished){ ;// send an intermediate activity report
along with the Logger's content
    GmailApp.sendEmail(Session.getEffectiveUser().getEmail(),
'inboxLabeller progress report', 'Still working, '+items+' processed
\n - see logger below \n \n'+Logger.getLog());
  }else{
    // if the task has completed, send a final report mail and delete
ScriptProperties and trigger
    GmailApp.sendEmail(Session.getEffectiveUser().getEmail(),
'inboxLabeller End report', 'Job completed : '+items+' processed');
    ScriptProperties.deleteAllProperties();
    var trigger = ScriptApp.getProjectTriggers()[0];
    ScriptApp.deleteTrigger(trigger);
  }
}


function getAds(tStart){
  var pub = GmailApp.getUserLabelByName('Ads');
  if(pub==null){
    pub = GmailApp.createLabel('Ads');// if you don't have an "Ads"
label then create it
  }
  var threads = GmailApp.search('category:promotions', tStart, 100);//
check the category Gmail added to the thread
  for(var n in threads){
    var tnr = Number(tStart)+Number(n);
```

```
    threads[n].addLabel(Ads);// move every message in the Ads folder/
label
    Logger.log('threads n° '+tnr+' = '+threads[n].
getFirstMessageSubject()+' has '+threads[n].getMessageCount()+'
messages ending on '+threads[n].getLastMessageDate());
    // show what we have done explicitly
  }
}
```

The following is a view of the message that the script will send every 10 minutes:

Creating e-mail messages

There are two Google services available to send e-mails: Gmail app and MailApp. The latter has only methods to send e-mails, while we have seen that Gmail app can do much more! When simply sending a message, we can use either of them interchangeably; I used to type MailApp more frequently but it is nothing more than a personal habit.

The basic process is really simple as described in the documentation (example taken from Google documentation page):

```
// Send an email with a file from Google Drive attached as a PDF.
 var file = DriveApp.getFileById('1234567890abcdefghijklmnopqrstuvwx
yz');
 GmailApp.sendEmail('mike@example.com', 'Attachment example', 'Please
see the attached file.', {
    attachments: [file.getAs(MimeType.PDF)],
    name: 'Automatic Emailer Script'
});
```

In the optional parameters, you can use some interesting values as follows:

- **Attachments**: These are an array of blobs (a blob is a data-interchange object for Apps Script services: https://developers.google.com/apps-script/reference/base/blob)

- **Cc, Bcc**, and **Reply-To**

- **Name**: This is the sender name as it will appear on screen

- **Inline images**

- **A no reply flag**: This will prevent the mail recipient from replying to the mail

- **The HTML content of the message**: This can be used as a value as the default content is plain text

To illustrate the HTML format, I'd suggest a code that we could use in our form example from the previous chapter by adding it to the form response spreadsheet. It will send us a report with the spreadsheet's content in a pleasant table format. We will provide a plain text version as well for people allergic to HTML-formatted e-mails.

I built the code using two separate functions—one to get data from the spreadsheet and send the mail, and a second one to actually compose the message body so that it will be much easier to re-use in another context:

```
function sendReport() {
  var ss = SpreadsheetApp.getActiveSpreadsheet();
  var formResp = ss.getSheetByName('Form Responses');// get the sheet
that contains data
  var data = formResp.getDataRange().getValues();// get all data in an
array of arrays aka 2D array)
  var htmlContent = createMsg(data)[0];// the function returns 2
results in an array, get the first one
  var textBody = createMsg(data)[1];// get the second one (text only,
tab separated items
  var htmlMsgObject = {'htmlBody' : htmlContent};// create an object
to use as optional parameter below
  GmailApp.sendEmail(Session.getActiveUser().getEmail(),'Daily report
of form responses',textBody,htmlMsgObject);// send to the active user
}

function createMsg(dataArray){
  var color='#CCF';// a blueish color for headers
```

```
var textMsg = 'Overview of last form responses :\n\n';// text title
var html = '<b>Overview of last form responses :</b><br><br><table
style="border-collapse:collapse;"border = 1 cellpadding = 5 >';// html
tags with styles
var table = '';
   for(var tt=0;tt<dataArray[0].length;tt++){
      table+= '<th valign="top" bgcolor="'+color+'"
cellpadding=5>'+dataArray[0][tt]+'</th>';
      textMsg+='\t'+dataArray[0][tt];
   };// first loop is for the headers
color='#FFC';// yellowish color for the table content
textMsg+='\n';
table+='</th><tr valign="middle" bgcolor="'+color+'"
cellpadding=5>';
for(var n=1;n<dataArray.length;n++){
   var row = dataArray[n];
   for(tt=0;tt<row.length;tt++){
      table+= '<td>'+row[tt]+'</td>';
      textMsg+='\t'+row[tt];
   };// second loop is for table items
   table+='</tr><tr valign="middle" bgcolor="'+color+'"
cellpadding=5>'  ;
textMsg+='\n';
}
table+='</tr></table>';
var msghtml = html+table;
textMsg+='\n';
Logger.log(msghtml);// check in the logger (optional)
Logger.log(textMsg);// check in the logger (optional)
return [msghtml,textMsg];// return 2 values in an array
}
```

The following screenshot shows an overview of last form responses:

Overview of last form responses :							
Timestamp	What is your last name ?	What are you ?	Do you prefer cars or dolls?	When were you born?	Rate your interests [Cars]	Rate your interests [Dolls]	Rate your interests [Food]
Fri Dec 27 2013 23:46:30 GMT+0100 (CET)	Serge	A man	Cars	Wed Feb 19 1958 09:00:00 GMT+0100 (CET)	annoying	no opinion	exciting
Sat Dec 28 2013 11:32:43 GMT+0100 (CET)	David	A man	computers	Wed Jun 25 1958 09:00:00 GMT+0100 (CET)	annoying	annoying	annoying

Let's admit that it looks more professional, doesn't it?

Automating a complete workflow

Now that we have discovered the most important methods available (not all of them, that's what the documentation is for), we can try and get our hands on the workflow that we suggested in the introductory example.

Just a reminder of that example is as follows:

You want to set up a filter that sets a label on every message coming from your boss, but you also want to keep an archive of it in a document along with a link to the attachments stored in your drive to be able to quickly search any reference he might have sent you. You would prefer that his e-mail messages remain in your main mailbox the whole day to be sure that you don't forget to read them.

I'm warning you, this code is a bit long.

When I imagined the example workflow, I thought it could be quite simple but some of the features need a lot of code lines, particularly the part that shows the attachment data in a table. I also wanted it to be simple to set up, so it creates the folders, the labels, the trigger to make it automatic, the filter to avoid double entries in log data; in one word, everything it needs to run in one single click.

This has an advantage; the code is not so simple but I have commented every part of it, so anyone can follow its logic.

Here it is. Starting with global variable definitions, there are style definitions too, which are shown at the end of the following code:

```
/* Global variables declaration
/  You should define the email address in this first variable
(theEmailOfYourBoss)
/  other parameters and variable are also defined as global variables
/  like the folderName and Gmail Label,
/  these can be customized to your need below
/  code should be embedded in a document.
*/
var theEmailOfYourBoss = 'example@example.com';
var boss = ScriptProperties.getProperty('bossEmail');
if(boss == null){ // test if email already exists
  ScriptProperties.setProperty('bossEmail',theEmailOfYourBoss);
}
var trigger = ScriptProperties.getProperty('bossEmailTrigger');
if(trigger == null){ // test if Trigger already exists
  var trigger =
    ScriptApp.newTrigger('takeCareOfTheseEmails').timeBased().
everyDays(1).atHour(2).create();
  ScriptProperties.setProperty('bossEmailTrigger',trigger.
getUniqueId());// save the trigger ID
```

```
}
var rootFolder = DriveApp.getRootFolder();
var Bossmails = GmailApp.getUserLabelByName('Boss-Emails');
if(Bossmails==null){
  // if you don't have an 'Boss-Emails' label then create it
  pub = GmailApp.createLabel('Boss-Emails');
}
var BossFolder = DriveApp.getFoldersByName('Boss_Files');
if(BossFolder.hasNext()){
  BossFolder = BossFolder.next();
}else{
  BossFolder = DriveApp.createFolder('Boss_Files');
}

// function starts here

function takeCareOfTheseEmails(){
  var doc = DocumentApp.getActiveDocument();// this document
  var body = doc.getBody();
  var inBoxThreads = GmailApp.getInboxThreads(0,100);
  // get the 100 most recent threads and loop into it
  for(var n=0;n<inBoxThreads.length;n++){
    var labelName = '';
    for(var l in inBoxThreads[n].getLabels())
{labelName+=inBoxThreads[n].getLabels()[l].getName()};
    Logger.log(labelName+' labelName.indexOf(Boss-Emails) =
'+labelName.indexOf('Boss-Emails')) ;
    if(labelName.indexOf('Boss-Emails')>-1){continue};
    var reject = false; // just a flag we use in the for loops
    // get the messages in each thread and store attachments in an
array
    var messages = inBoxThreads[n].getMessages();
    for(var m=0;m<messages.length;m++){
      var attach = [];
      // get the sender email and check if it comes from the boss
      var sender = messages[m].getFrom();
      if(sender.indexOf(boss)===-1){reject = true};
      if(reject){n++; break };
      inBoxThreads[n].addLabel(Bossmails);
      // get message date, subject, attachments and body
      var msgDate = Utilities.formatDate(messages[m].getDate(),
Session.getTimeZone(),'MM-dd-yyyy @HH:mm');
      var msgSubject = messages[m].getSubject();
      var attachments = messages[m].getAttachments();
      var msgBody = messages[m].getBody();
      var msgBodyDocHtml = DriveApp.createFile('msg received on
'+msgDate,msgBody,MimeType.HTML);
      // move the file to its folder and remove it from 'my drive'
      BossFolder.addFile(msgBodyDocHtml);
```

```
    rootFolder.removeFile(msgBodyDocHtml);
    // get the corresponding blob if we want to send it as
attachment, get the thumbnail if exists
    var bodyDocUrl=msgBodyDocHtml.getUrl();
    var msgBodyBlob = msgBodyDocHtml.getBlob();
    var msgBodyDocThumb = msgBodyDocHtml.getThumbnail();
    // retrieve a text version of the message and keep only the 400
first characters
    var textSummary = getTextFromHtml(msgBody);
    var length = (textSummary.length <400 ? textSummary.length :
400);
    textSummary = textSummary.substr(0,length)+'..............';
    var attSize = 0;
    var attName = 'no attachment';
    var attUrl = '---';
    // define a header for attachment display
    attach.push(['attachment name','attachment Size','attachment
url']);
    for(var a in attachments){
       // get the size, name and URL of the attachment
      attSize = attachments[a].getSize()+' bytes';
      attName = '/Boss_Files/'+attachments[a].getName();
      attUrl = BossFolder.createFile(attachments[a]).getUrl();
      // store file/name and size in an array
      attach.push([attName,attSize,attUrl]);
    }
    body.appendParagraph('Thread Nr '+n+', Message nr '+m+'\rReceived
on '+msgDate+' from '
        +sender.split('<')[0]+' with Subject : "'+msgSubject+'"\
rStarting with : \r'+textSummary).setAttributes(bodyStyle);
    // show a link to the message stored in drive and show thumbnail
& attachment name if exist
    body.appendParagraph('View here').setLinkUrl(bodyDocUrl);
    if(msgBodyDocThumb){body.appendImage(msgBodyDocThumb)};
    if(attach.length>1){
      var table = body.appendTable(attach).
setAttributes(tableStyle).setBorderColor('#aaaaaa');
      for(var r = 0 ; r<table.getNumRows() ; r++){
        var row = table.getRow(r);
        for(var c = 0 ; c < row.getNumCells(); c++){
          var cell = row.getCell(c).setAttributes(cellStyle);
          }
      }
    }
    body.appendHorizontalRule();
  }
 }
 // flush all changes and save the doc
 doc.saveAndClose();
}
```

```
// this function borrowed from stackoverflow contributor Corey G
function getTextFromHtml(html) {
  return getTextFromNode(Xml.parse(html, true).getElement());
}

function getTextFromNode(x) {
  switch(x.toString()) {
    case 'XmlText': return x.toXmlString();
    case 'XmlElement': return x.getNodes().map(getTextFromNode).
join('');
    default: return '';
  }
}

// style definitions as global variables
  var tableStyle = {};// define a tyle for table
  tableStyle[DocumentApp.Attribute.FONT_SIZE] = 8;
  tableStyle[DocumentApp.Attribute.FONT_FAMILY] =DocumentApp.
FontFamily.ARIAL_NARROW;
  tableStyle[DocumentApp.Attribute.FOREGROUND_COLOR] = "#FF5555";
  tableStyle[DocumentApp.Attribute.BORDER_WIDTH] = 0.5;
  var bodyStyle = {};// define a style for body
  bodyStyle[DocumentApp.Attribute.FONT_SIZE] = 10;
  bodyStyle[DocumentApp.Attribute.FONT_FAMILY] = DocumentApp.
FontFamily.ARIAL;
  bodyStyle[DocumentApp.Attribute.FOREGROUND_COLOR] = "#555555";
  bodyStyle[DocumentApp.Attribute.MARGIN_LEFT] = 20;
  bodyStyle[DocumentApp.Attribute.MARGIN_BOTTOM] = 20;
  bodyStyle[DocumentApp.Attribute.MARGIN_RIGHT] = 20;
  bodyStyle[DocumentApp.Attribute.MARGIN_TOP] = 20;
  var cellStyle = {};// define a style for cells individually
  cellStyle[DocumentApp.Attribute.PADDING_BOTTOM] = 0;
  cellStyle[DocumentApp.Attribute.PADDING_TOP] = 5;
  cellStyle[DocumentApp.Attribute.PADDING_LEFT] = 5;
  cellStyle[DocumentApp.Attribute.PADDING_RIGHT] = 0;
  cellStyle[DocumentApp.Attribute.HEIGHT] = 15;
// end of file
```

This code has to be pasted in a new text document script's editor (this was also a motivation behind writing this example; now we know that the text document also has scripts) and run once.

 Before running the code, please choose a valid e-mail address for the theEmailOfYourBoss variable (first uncommented line in the preceding code).

It will ask for the usual authorizations and begin to work.

Every night, between 2 a.m. and 3 a.m., it will execute again and examine the 100 most recent threads; if ever it's not enough for your use case, you can change it easily in line 24 by changing `100` to a bigger value:

```
var inBoxThreads = GmailApp.getInboxThreads(0,100);// get the 100
most recent threads
```

Just keep in mind that the total execution time cannot exceed five minutes, so don't ask for 5000 threads; I'm afraid they won't work and if you receive that many e-mails, I guess you should quit your job—too much pressure for sure!

Thread Nr 0, Message nr 0
Received on 12-29-2013 @23:13 from ▓▓▓▓▓ with Subject : "another test"
Starting with :

Getting Started with Apps ScriptGetting Started with Apps ScriptGetting Started with Apps ScriptGetting Started with Apps ScriptGetting Started with Apps ScriptGetting Started with Apps ScriptGetting Started with Apps ScriptGetting Started with Apps ScriptGetting Started with Apps ScriptGetting Started with Apps ScriptGetting Started with Apps ScriptGetting Started with Apps ScriptGetting Started with Apps ScriptGetting Started.............

View here

attachment name	attachment Size	attachment url
/Boss_Files/capture 2013-12-28 à 13.14.48.JPG	30805 bytes	https://docs.google.com/file/d/0B3qSFd3ikE3aHFPN1Bl ZkpDZVk/edit?usp=drivesdk
/Boss_Files/capture 2013-12-28 à 12.57.07.JPG	33525 bytes	https://docs.google.com/file/d/0B3qSFd3ikE3UnNkbXVP djd3Wms/edit?usp=drivesdk
/Boss_Files/capture 2013-12-28 à 12.44.46.JPG	26882 bytes	https://docs.google.com/file/d/0B3qSFd3ikE3SEY5SUxs QTRBRTQ/edit?usp=drivesdk

---

Summary

In this chapter, we saw that the Gmail service offers an impressive range of methods that allow for almost any possible manipulation of your mailbox content.

Anything that you can do manually but would take a long time to achieve can be done using script, and as this boss' e-mail example shows you, you can even imagine other scenarios without difficulty. Let Google Apps Script do your work for you.

This latter example also gave us an opportunity to use the document service and this will be the main point of interest in the next chapter.

4
Embedding Scripts in Text Documents

In the previous chapter, through the example of compiling the boss' e-mails, we learned that Google documents can have embedded scripts just like spreadsheets or forms do.

This example use case could well have been implemented in a spreadsheet and in some aspects, it probably would have been easier, but the reason was more an aesthetic choice; in spreadsheets there is an absence of grid and cell limitations and the ability to customize the appearance with styles and colors.

That is only a small example of what can be done in Google documents.

What can be done

If we consider the way these online documents work "behind the scenes", that is, the functioning of the backend software that Google has put in place to allow real-time editing and sharing, we shouldn't be surprised that a part of it has become available to Apps Script programmers.

Remember that the file we are about to manipulate will not be hosted on our computer, but somewhere on Google's servers. The page we actually see is nothing but the rendering of a set of instructions that we sent to this server. Each keystroke, paragraph, or format we change may be considered as a small code sent to the server running an application.

Of course, we don't need to know all of them. The engineers who designed the Google Docs service API had to translate it in a JavaScript-compliant language that anyone could use.

A look at the available methods at `https://developers.google.com/apps-script/reference/document` will tell you more about the plethora of methods than a description in this book ever could, even if I had a 100 pages to fill.

So, let us focus on a couple of pleasant features illustrated with practical examples in the following sections.

Generating a Google document from spreadsheet data using a script

I mentioned earlier that we could have used a spreadsheet in the previous Gmail example to log the data we retrieved from the e-mail messages, but that the document approach was more pleasant in terms of "look". So I suggest that we try to build a Google document from data stored in a spreadsheet.

The data can be a list of addresses or recipes. It doesn't really matter what data we use as the methods we use will be the same, but we'll use the list of recipes because they have pictures in them and had might as well give you some ideas for your next weekend lunch.

The following screenshot shows how our current data sheet looks—it's not very elegant:

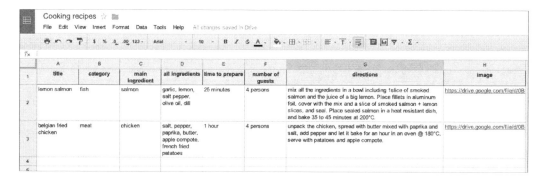

We already know how to get data from a spreadsheet (see *Chapter 1, Enhancing Spreadsheets*) and that using `getValues()` will return an array of arrays with all the cells' data in a raw format.

Each row will be an array of values corresponding to each cell; these arrays will in turn be wrapped in an array. We also see in our example that the first row in the sheet has headers that we may want to use to get the structure of the data.

Speaking of structure, if you read the tutorials on Google's help page (`https://developers.google.com/apps-script/articles`), you have probably noticed that they use a method to get data from a spreadsheet as objects, with the object of each row having its cell properties labelled using header values (`https://developers.google.com/apps-script/guides/sheets#reading`).

There are actually many ways to manipulate data from spreadsheets. A **Two-Dimensional (2D)** array (in other words, an array of arrays) is a pleasant one. JavaScript-named objects are also nice to use and I have no real opinion about which is best, so I suggest that this time we give the object method a try. The next time will use pure array manipulation. Both approaches begin the same way: select a range in the sheet and get its values, then isolate the headers to know what data it has. This is done using the following code:

```
var data = SpreadsheetApp.getActive().getDataRange().getValues();
var headers = data.shift();
```

The preceding code results in the following output:

Logging output

[14-01-22 17:09:54:637 CET] data array = German lemon salmon,fish,salmon,garlic, lemon, salt pepper, olive oil, dill,25 minutes,4 persons, mix all the ingredients in a bowl including 1 slice of smoked salmon and the juice of a big lemon. Place fillets in aluminum foil, cover with the mix and a slice of smoked salmon + lemon slices, and seal. Place sealed salmon in a heat resistant dish, and bake 35 to 45 minutes at 200°C.,https://drive.google.com/file/d/0B3qSFd3iikE3UmpjelRQdlZmQXc/edit?usp=sharing,Belgian fried chicken,meat,chicken,salt, pepper, paprika, butter, apple compote, french fried potatoes,1 hour,4 persons,unpack the chicken, spread with butter mixed with paprika and salt, add pepper and let it bake for an hour in an oven @ 180°C, serve with potatoes and apple compote.,https://drive.google.com/file/d/0B3qSFd3iikE3N2ZWSzZmelM4WWc/edit?usp=sharing
[14-01-22 17:09:54:637 CET] headers array = Recipe title,Meal category,main ingredient,all ingredients,time to prepare,number of guests,directions,image url

---

 var data contains all the cells in an array of arrays. The shift() method removes the first array (which is equal to the first row) and assigns it to var headers. See the example documentation from w3schools at the following link:

`http://www.w3schools.com/jsref/jsref_shift.asp`

That is the common part of the two approaches. From now on, we must change our script to get JavaScript objects. As explained in the Google tutorial, it is advisable to use a CamelCase format for the object's variable names. It suggests a script to do so, but we're going to try something else, such as playing with a few string and array methods. See the comments in the following code and use the Logger to see every step of the process:

```
function camelise(stringArray) {
  var camelised = [];// this will hold the function result
  for(var n in stringArray){
    Logger.log('title original = '+stringArray[n])
    var title = stringArray[n].replace(/\W/gi,' ').split(' ');
    // replace every non "word" char with space and split string into
an array (split on space)
    Logger.log('title array alphanumeric only = '+title)
    var result = '';
    for(var t in title){
      if(title[t].replace(/ /g,'')==''){ continue };
      // skip any empty field
      result+=title[t].replace(/ /g,'')+'|';
      // compose a result string with | separators (easier to see in
the Logger) and no spaces
    }
    title = result.toLowerCase().split('|');
    // everything in lowercase and convert back to an array splitting
on | separators
    var camelCase = '';// initialize the result string
    for(t=0 ; t<title.length-1 ; t++){
    // let's handle each word separately, the first word (index 0)
should remain unchanged
      if(t==0){
        var capWord = title[t];
      }else{
        capWord = title[t].substring(0,1).toUpperCase()+title[t].
substr(1);
      } // every following item gets a capital first letter
      camelCase+=capWord;// compose output result
    }
    // view each result in the Logger and store in an array
    Logger.log('camelCase = '+camelCase);
    camelised.push(camelCase);
  }
  // return the array of headers in CamelCase format
  return camelised;
}
```

Now we can test the preceding code using a special temporary function such as the one in the following code snippet:

```
function testGetHeadersAsCamelCase(){
    var data = SpreadsheetApp.getActive().getDataRange().getValues();//
we get all the cells with data in one call
    var headers = data.shift();// the first row is headers row and we
remove this row from data altogether
    var ccHeaders = camelise(headers);
    for(var n in headers){ // create a loop
        Logger.log(headers[n]+' becomes >> '+ccHeaders[n]);
    }
}
```

So we get the following partial log:

```
..........
[13-12-31 09:16:19:385 CET] Recipe title becomes >> recipeTitle
[13-12-31 09:16:19:385 CET] Meal category becomes >> mealCategory
[13-12-31 09:16:19:386 CET] main ingredient becomes >> mainIngredient
[13-12-31 09:16:19:386 CET] all ingredients becomes >> allIngredients
[13-12-31 09:16:19:386 CET] time to prepare becomes >> timeToPrepare
[13-12-31 09:16:19:386 CET] number of guests becomes >> numberOfGuests
[13-12-31 09:16:19:387 CET] directions becomes >> directions
[13-12-31 09:16:19:387 CET] image url becomes >> imageUrl
```

Now that we have our headers in the right format, that is CamelCase, we can read the data in the sheet using the headers as keys and each cell row as value to build JavaScript Objects with key:value pairs as properties; the following code snippet depicts this:

```
function getObjects(data, keys) {
    var objects = [];// create an empty array variable
    for (var i = 0; i < data.length; ++i) {// iterate sheet data
        var object = {};
// create an empty "object" variable and then iterate each row's
content
        for (var j = 0; j < data[i].length; ++j) {
            var cellData = data[i][j];
// check if cell is empty or contains any white space
            if (cellData.toString().replace(/ /g,'')=='') {
                continue;
            }else{
                object[keys[j]] = cellData;// assign value to key
            }
        }
```

```
        objects.push(object);//store every object in array
    }
    return objects;
}
```

Create a new document to hold the values as shown in the following piece of code:

```
var docId = DocumentApp.create('Recipes in a doc').getId();
Logger.log(docId);
```

We use another function to populate the document with text, tables, and images. In this chapter, I have called this function exportToDoc(docId,objects,keys, headers). It has four parameters: the newly created document ID, the array of objects, the keys (in case we need them), and the headers to show field information.

The next part of the code is not very hard to read. The various style definitions are defined as global variables at the end of the script as usual, but the data handling itself is very simple, thanks to the array-of-objects structure.

The document formatting function is reproduced in the following code with comments on the important parts:

```
function exportToDoc(docId,objects,keys,headers){
  var doc = DocumentApp.openById(docId);
  var body = doc.getBody();
  var docHeader = doc.addHeader().appendParagraph('My favourite
recipes\rCreated by script on '
                  +Utilities.formatDate(new Date(), Session.
getTimeZone(),'MMM dd @ HH:mm'));
  // use the style defined outside of the function and use an
alignment setting
  docHeader.setAttributes(styleHeader).setAlignment(DocumentApp.
HorizontalAlignment.CENTER);
  for(var n in objects){
    body.appendParagraph('An idea for a meal with '+objects[n]
[keys[1]]+' composed mainly of '+objects[n][keys[2]]+' for
'+objects[n][keys[5]]+' :').setAttributes(styleBase);
    body.appendParagraph('The name of this recipe is "'+objects[n]
[keys[0]]+'" but I invented it myself \rso you can change it if you
want').setAttributes(styleBase);
    body.appendHorizontalRule();
    body.appendParagraph('List of '+headers[3]+' :');
    var table = [];
    var ing = objects[n][keys[3]].split(',');
    for(var i in ing){ table.push(['You must have '+ ing[i]]) };
```

```
    body.appendTable(table).setAttributes(styleTable);
    body.appendParagraph('Try to get some free time, it will take
approximately '+objects[n][keys[4]]+', then clean up your kitchen and
'+objects[n][keys[6]]).setAttributes(styleDirections);
    body.appendHorizontalRule();
    var image = DriveApp.getFileById(objects[n][keys[7]].split('d/')
[1].split('/')[0]).getBlob();// retrieve ID from URL
    // https://drive.google.com/file/d/0B3qSFd3iikE3UmpjelRQdlZmQXc/
edit?usp=sharing This is a typical link
    body.appendParagraph('good apetite ;) ').appendInlineImage(image).
setWidth(300).setHeight(200).getParent().setAttributes(styleImage);
    body.appendHorizontalRule();
    if(n<objects.length){body.appendPageBreak()};
  }
}
```

The style definitions are grouped at the end of the script. They can even be stored in a separate script file within the same project. This is shown in the following code snippet:

```
// Style definitions as global variables
  var bodyStyle = {};// define a style for body, margin etc...
  bodyStyle[DocumentApp.Attribute.MARGIN_LEFT] = 30;
  bodyStyle[DocumentApp.Attribute.MARGIN_BOTTOM] = 20;
  bodyStyle[DocumentApp.Attribute.MARGIN_RIGHT] = 30;
  bodyStyle[DocumentApp.Attribute.MARGIN_TOP] = 20;
  body.setAttributes(bodyStyle);
  var styleBase = {};// a "base" style for paragraphs
  styleBase[DocumentApp.Attribute.FONT_SIZE] = 11;
  styleBase[DocumentApp.Attribute.FONT_FAMILY] = DocumentApp.
FontFamily.AMARANTH;
  styleBase[DocumentApp.Attribute.FOREGROUND_COLOR] = "#444400";
  var styleHeader = {};// define a style for document header
  styleHeader[DocumentApp.Attribute.BACKGROUND_COLOR] = '#eeeeff'
  styleHeader[DocumentApp.Attribute.FONT_SIZE] = 16;
  styleHeader[DocumentApp.Attribute.FONT_FAMILY] = DocumentApp.
FontFamily.CORSIVA;
  styleHeader[DocumentApp.Attribute.FOREGROUND_COLOR] = '#0000aa';
  var styleTable = {};// define a style for table
  styleTable[DocumentApp.Attribute.FONT_SIZE] = 10;
  styleTable[DocumentApp.Attribute.FONT_FAMILY] =DocumentApp.
FontFamily.AMARANTH;
  styleTable[DocumentApp.Attribute.FOREGROUND_COLOR] = "#005500";
  styleTable[DocumentApp.Attribute.BORDER_WIDTH] = 0 ;
```

```
var styleDirections = {};// define a style for direction paragraph
styleDirections[DocumentApp.Attribute.FONT_SIZE] = 12;
styleDirections[DocumentApp.Attribute.FONT_FAMILY] = DocumentApp.
FontFamily.CONSOLAS;
styleDirections[DocumentApp.Attribute.ITALIC] = true;
styleDirections[DocumentApp.Attribute.FOREGROUND_COLOR] = "#000066";
var styleImage = {};
styleImage[DocumentApp.Attribute.HORIZONTAL_ALIGNMENT] =
DocumentApp.HorizontalAlignment.CENTER;
// end of file
```

We can now write a main function that will call all the others in turn; the function `generateDoc()` will be the one to call to create the document as shown in the following code snippet:

```
function generateDoc(){
  var data = SpreadsheetApp.getActive().getDataRange().getValues();
  // we first get all the cells with data in one call
  var headers = data.shift();
  // shift is an array function the removes the first row
  // and assign it to the variable headers
  var keys = getHeadersAsCamelCase(headers);
  // get the CamelCase formatted headers using a separate function
  var objects = getObjects(data, keys);
  for(var n in objects){
    for(var k in keys){
      Logger.log('Object '+n+' properties '+keys[k]+' = '+objects[n]
[keys[k]]);
    }
  }
  // we get all the values using 2 loops
  var docId = DocumentApp.create('Recipes in a doc').getId();
  //create a doc as a container for our recipes
  Logger.log(docId);
  exportToDoc(docId,objects,keys,headers);
}
```

Running `generateDoc()` is going to create a multipage document with one recipe per page with a better layout and an inline image.

The next step would be to create a form linked to the source spreadsheet (as seen in *Chapter 2, Create and Manipulate Forms*) so that all your friends can add their own recipes. With a single click, you will be ready to publish a cookbook with no effort. If you do, just let me know, I love cooking!

The following screenshot shows the document created:

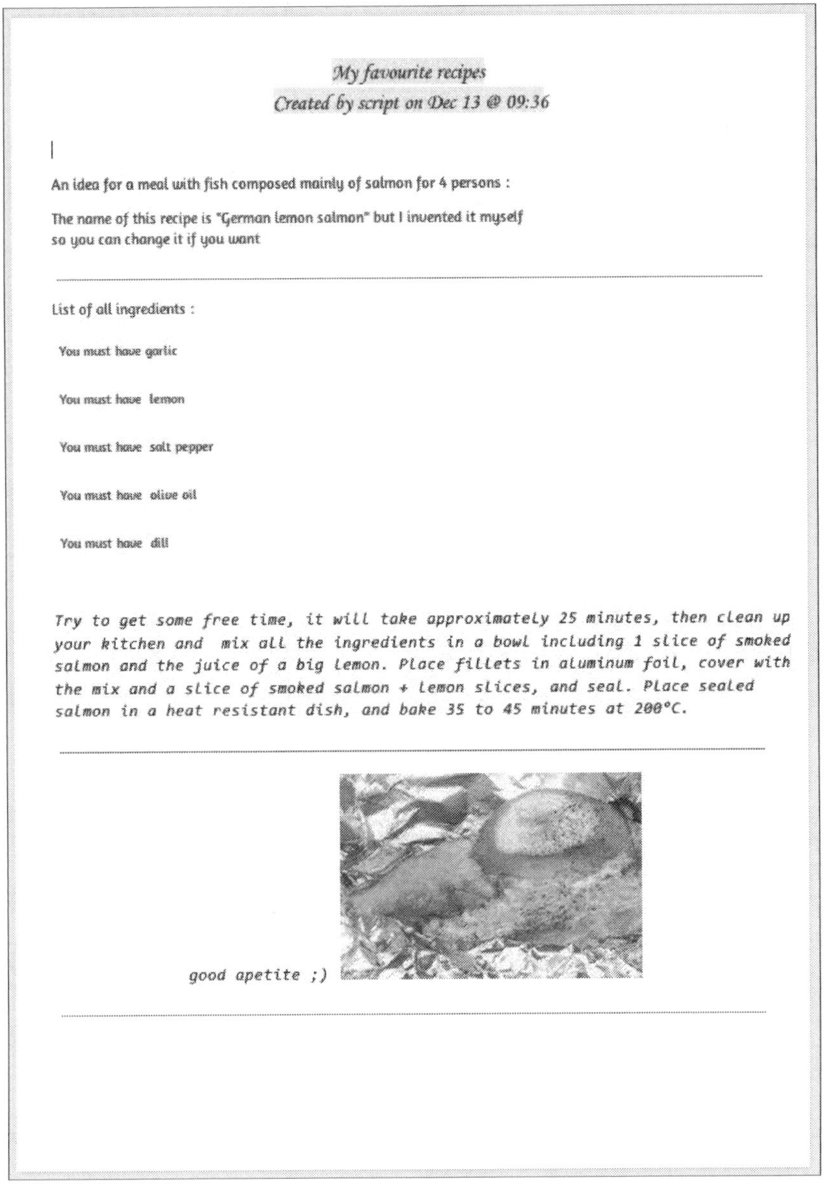

My favourite recipes
Created by script on Dec 13 @ 09:36

An idea for a meal with fish composed mainly of salmon for 4 persons :

The name of this recipe is "German lemon salmon" but I invented it myself so you can change it if you want

List of all ingredients :

You must have garlic

You must have lemon

You must have salt pepper

You must have olive oil

You must have dill

Try to get some free time, it will take approximately 25 minutes, then clean up your kitchen and mix all the ingredients in a bowl including 1 slice of smoked salmon and the juice of a big lemon. Place fillets in aluminum foil, cover with the mix and a slice of smoked salmon + lemon slices, and seal. Place sealed salmon in a heat resistant dish, and bake 35 to 45 minutes at 200°C.

good apetite ;)

Analyzing, duplicating, and modifying document elements

In the first section of this chapter, we have built a document from scratch using various methods, but we could also try the reverse process; in other words, we can analyze a document to see its content.

In doing so, we will be able to copy a part of the document, modify the document's content, and even insert new elements in the document or simply assemble multiple documents in one (see, for example, my last answer on this post at `http://stackoverflow.com/questions/10939031/how-to-delete-blank-pages-in-a-multipage-`).

Just about every method set in `DocumentApp` has a symmetric `get` method that returns precise information on every element. Elements can be built hierarchically with parents and children (I used that hierarchy when inserting the image in our example; the image was a child of the paragraph : `body.appendParagraph('good apetite').appendInlineImage(image)` and a good analyze script will have to examine elements at every level.

Using a script to insert an image into a document

A complete example including every method would be very long, so I'll show a simplified layout to show how it works, but that only identifies every type of element and replaces a paragraph with an image if a predefined placeholder `=='###'`, is found in the paragraph.

You should easily be able to implement a more universal version yourself that adds or modifies elements based on certain conditions. Test the following code in a text document, such as the one we just created with our recipes.

```
function findMarkAndReplace() {
  var Doc = DocumentApp.getActiveDocument();
  var image = DocsList.getFileById('0B3qSFd3iikE3UmpjelRQdlZmQXc');
  // this is an image from the recipe's example stored on my drive and
shared publicly
  var totalElements = Doc.getNumChildren();
  var el=[];
  for( var j = 0; j < totalElements; ++j ) {
    var element = Doc.getChild(j);
    var type = element.getType();
    Logger.log('element '+j+" : "+type);
    // to see doc's content type
```

```
    if (type =='PARAGRAPH'){
      el[j]=element.getText();
      if(el[j]=='###'){
        element.removeFromParent();
        // remove the ### placeholder
        Doc.insertImage(j, image);
        // 'image' is the image file as blob
      }
    }
  }
}
}
```

Compiling and presenting data from other services

In the example we used to create a document, we were getting data from a spreadsheet; but, of course, you can get data from any other Google service and, although it is not as simple, any other data server on the Internet. This is one of the major advantages of the document creation mode that Google has implemented in this service.

Just about anything that contains text can be imported and presented in a Google document along with images, drawings, and even math formulas. The preceding example showed how to insert an image stored in our drive; the next one will get text from our personal calendar.

Calendar, contact, spreadsheets, and forms are really easy to get data from in a way that fits pretty well in a text document, because every property can be obtained as a string. It is only a matter of imagination and creativity on your part to concatenate everything in a pleasant way.

The following is a very basic example of a script that gets events from your default calendar and writes them in an open document. I haven't used any style parameters apart from background color and horizontal alignment to keep it as short as possible:

```
function importFromCal(){
  var cal = CalendarApp.getDefaultCalendar();
  var endDate = new Date();
  var startDate = new Date(endDate.getTime()-30*24*3600000);
  // start date is 30 days before end date
  var events = cal.getEvents(startDate, endDate);
  var doc = DocumentApp.getActiveDocument();
  var body = doc.getBody();
  var styleEvent = {};
  //define a style object to play with
  for(var n=0 ; n<events.length; n++){
```

```
   if( n % 2 == 0){
 // every odd row will be right aligned, every even row will be left
aligned
     styleEvent[DocumentApp.Attribute.HORIZONTAL_ALIGNMENT] =
DocumentApp.HorizontalAlignment.LEFT;
   }else{
     styleEvent[DocumentApp.Attribute.HORIZONTAL_ALIGNMENT] =
DocumentApp.HorizontalAlignment.RIGHT;
   }
   var bgColor = parseInt(0xff*(n+1)/events.length);
   // fade color to white using hex values
   Logger.log('color = #'+bgColor.toString(16)+'ffff');
   styleEvent[DocumentApp.Attribute.FOREGROUND_COLOR] = '#222222';
   styleEvent[DocumentApp.Attribute.BACKGROUND_COLOR] = '#'+bgColor.
toString(16)+'ffff';
   body.appendParagraph(events[n].getTitle()+'\r'+events[n].
getDescription()+'\ron '+Utilities.formatDate(events[n].
getStartTime(), Session.getTimeZone(),'MMM dd, yyyy')+'\r@'+events[n].
getLocation()).setAttributes(styleEvent);
   }
}
```

The following screenshot shows the result of the preceding code:

In the preceding code, we used some pure JavaScript methods such as `Math.floor` and `%` that are well explained on many JavaScript reference websites (for example, `https://developer.mozilla.org/en-US/docs/Web/JavaScript/Reference/Global_Objects/Math`).

Spend some time reading the documentation about all the elements that you can include in a document and all the data sources you can use.

In the next chapter, we will use a document embedded in a Google website and update it automatically everyday with data from a spreadsheet.

Summary

Document-embedded scripts can be used on many different occasions; we have seen how to build or change the content of a document and analyze what is already in it; this process could easily be developed to create an elegant mail-merge workflow, getting data directly from your Gmail contact.

In *Chapter 7, Using User Interfaces in Spreadsheets and Documents*, we'll see that we can also add a custom user interface to a document and create new features that make the documents even more attractive and efficient. In the next chapter, we will learn about embedding scripts on Google sites.

5
Embedding Scripts in Google Sites

As you probably know, Google Sites is a free service included in every Google account that allows the creation of Google websites. These free websites have a URL such as `https://sites.google.com/site/siteName/pageName`, but if you have a Google Apps account (education or business) and a domain, you will be able to customize this URL and even create e-mail accounts with an `@domain.xxx` address.

We are going to consider only the standard accounts without domains as they will be use cases for most of us, and Google Apps for business is a subject for another book on its own.

This means that some methods will be unavailable; if that is the case, the documentation will always mention it clearly (`https://developers.google.com/apps-script/reference/sites/sites-app`).

To start with creating a site, log in to your Google account and go to the URL `https://sites.google.com/site/` that will show you all your current sites, if you have some, and suggest that you should create one if you don't have any.

There are two main features of Google Apps Script with regard to Google Sites as follows:

- You can build a so-called "gadget" that you can insert into a site page, which will more or less work as usual web applications do
- You can use Google Scripts to create or modify the site's content itself

The first aspect about standalone web applications will be examined in more detail in the next chapter since it uses the same services (UiApp and HTML services), but let us have a quick peek at a simple example.

Site gadget's limitations/restrictions/use cases

Site-embedded web applications are a nice way to give access to your script functions because they enable easy page navigation and the possibility to add descriptions, directions for use, and illustrations, making your apps easier for other users to use.

If we think about the very first script example in *Chapter 1, Enhancing Spreadsheets,* that calculated my age in hours and that we tried in a spreadsheet, the same script modified to work as a site gadget would be much more fun and easy to make public without us needing to share any access to any of our documents. Moreover, even a user having no experience with spreadsheets would be able to use it without difficulty.

The code will need to be changed to create a small and basic user interface so that users can enter their birth date and time. This requires a few methods and a workflow, which we haven't talked about yet (it is for the next chapter), but for now you can simply copy it and follow the instructions and leave the "understanding" bit for later!

The code has two parts: one part that creates the user interface to enter values and a second that retrieves the values, does the calculations, and shows the result in the same UI.

The first part of the code is as follows; simply copy it as it is:

```
function doGet() {
 var app = UiApp.createApplication().setTitle('Age In Hours');
 var grid = app.createGrid(3,2);
 var handler = app.createServerHandler('myAgeInHours').
addCallbackElement(grid);
 var time = app.createListBox().setName('time').addItem('Choose the
hour',-1);
 for(var n=0 ; n<24 ; n++){time.addItem(n+' h',n)};
 var date = app.createDateBox().setName('date');
 var button = app.createButton('Show me...',handler);
grid.setWidget(0,0,date).setWidget(0,1,time).setWidget(1,0,button);
 app.add(grid);
 return app;
}
```

And the part we took from our aforementioned example has a few modifications: the birth date was a predefined string and is now a pair of user-created values (the date and time) that we get from the UI; and the date value (`var date`) has an hour value equal to 0 because the widget returns a value at midnight (00:00 Hrs), so we need to subtract the separate hour value from the result (`var time` that we get from the UI too, and convert it to a number) to get the count correctly.

The second part of the code is as follows:

```
function myAgeInHours(e){
 var app = UiApp.getActiveApplication();
 var myBirthDate = e.parameter.date.getTime();// the returned value
for date (in milliseconds)
 var time = Number(e.parameter.time) == - 1 ? 0 : Number(e.parameter.
time);// the returned value in hours combined with a condition
 myBirthDate = parseInt(myBirthDate/3600000, 10);
 var today = parseInt(new Date().getTime()/3600000, 10);
 app.add(app.createLabel().setText('there are '+(today-myBirthDate-
time)+' hours between now and your birth date !'));// write the result
in a 'label'
 return app; // this tells the script to update the UI
}
```

If you don't feel like going through the whole process of publishing this script to get it as a web application that you can embed in your site (and I recommend that you either do this or read the next chapter before going further), you can simply use the URL of my copy that I have shared publicly at https://script.google.com/ macros/s/AKfycbzB3J4BiI8E6IjuT3ddZOnpTL-0HhklULeLAzZ2jZnFDWHQA8q3/ exec and insert it as a gadget on your site. There are, indeed, two ways to add a script gadget to a web page: by pasting the URL of a published (deployed) web app or writing the code in the site page's embedded script editor. In the latter case, it will be listed as a suggestion, but in both cases, the app has to be deployed first.

If you try to use the `< insert script >` tag from the page editor of your site without publishing beforehand, you'll see that error panel from Google telling you the file you requested does not exist, as shown in the following screenshot:

This seems logical since it looked for the HTML rendering of your script and not its text version.

Choosing between standalone apps and site-embedded, document-embedded, and spreadsheet-embedded scripts is really a matter of choice and depends mainly on how you will need to have or give access to the application.

In Google Sites, you can define authorizations and rights at two levels: on the site and at the page level. To manage access at the page level, you must activate the feature, and this will show you the warning **Page-level permissions allow you to set different levels of access for different people on different pages. For example, you could allow all your friends to see one set of pages, allow your family to edit another set of pages, and then keep yet another set of pages private only to yourself..**

We can learn more about page-level permissions at the following link:

```
https://support.google.com/sites/answer/1387384?ref_
topic=1387383&rd=1
```

This is a very powerful feature that you can use when sharing a project with different people as you may have editors and readers/testers that have different access to different parts of the site.

 This is a hierarchical construction; each page you create under a shared page inherits from the parent's shared settings.

We'll see in the next section that these settings can be adjusted programmatically.

Also keep in mind that the sharing setting of the site is not linked to the authorization of the script. If you share a web page with an embedded script and forget to share the access to this app, the guest user won't be able to run it.

We will see more details on how to set up app access with standalone apps.

Creating and maintaining sites with Google Apps Script

As mentioned earlier, script gadgets are only a small part of Google Sites; the interesting feature of Apps Script in Google Sites is its ability to create and modify the site itself with a script.

Imagine you have a site for your restaurant and that you publish a new menu every day that follows a predefined scenario: pasta on Monday, beef on Tuesday, and so on. You would normally edit your menu page at the end of the day so that it is updated every morning with the right menu. This is a typical example of an annoying repetitive task that a script could easily do for you.

Create all of the daily menu's contents in some document, maybe a spreadsheet. For example, take the time to create a nice-looking template in a Google document and write a script that will update the site automatically every night based on the template and the spreadsheet data.

This might seem hard to do, but we'll use methods that we've already tried and proceed step-by-step. Refer to the following code:

```
// Document Ids as global variables
var sharedDocID = '1f4uW-0l3xsmQspsseipDcHIw_mUC1kpEQ6Js7rhFUxk'
var sharedSpreadSheetID = '1Sa9Mah6eFbjZBEq5t0GtyMo_NjHZfnJ-
SXwW409xUD8'

function updateSite() {
 var ss = SpreadsheetApp.openById(sharedSpreadSheetID);
 var sh = ss.getSheetByName('Sheet1');
 var data = sh.getDataRange().getValues();
 var headers = data.shift();// Monday Tuesday Wednesday Thursday
Friday Saturday Sunday
 var todayInSheet = new Date().getDay() == 0 ? 7 : new Date().
getDay();// in JS Monday is 1 and Sunday is 0 so we need a bit of
logic there
 var menuData = [];// the actual meal
 var menuTitle = [];// starter, main course...
 for(var n=0 ; n<data.length ; n++){
   menuData.push(data[n][todayInSheet]);
   menuTitle.push(data[n][0]);
 }
 Logger.log('\ndata = '+menuData+'\nTitle = '+menuTitle);
```

This first part simply reads the data from the spreadsheet, and instead of creating JS objects, we simply keep array elements. The spreadsheet ID is hardcoded in the script; you should modify this with the ID of your own spreadsheet.

```
var menuFolder = DriveApp.getFoldersByName('Menu online');
if(menuFolder.hasNext()){
  var menuFolder = menuFolder.next();
}else{
  menuFolder = DriveApp.createFolder('Menu online');
}
```

This code has already been used in the Boss mail example in *Chapter 3, Managing an E-mail Account*; if the folder already exists then use it, or create it to store the temporary document that contains daily data. This is shown in the preceding code.

```
var docCopy = DriveApp.getFileById(sharedDocID).makeCopy('menu['+heade
rs[todayInSheet]+']');
  menuFolder.addFile(docCopy);
  DriveApp.getRootFolder().removeFile(docCopy);
```

We get the document's template through its ID (it is hardcoded here again, so you should change it to the value from your document). We copy the template to the folder and remove it from My Drive. We have to do so because there is no move method for files in Google Script. The preceding code snippet depicts this.

```
var docCopyId = docCopy.getId();
  if(ScriptProperties.getProperty('docCopyId')!=null){
var fileToDelete = DriveApp.getFileById(ScriptProperties.
getProperty('docCopyId')).setTrashed(true);// delete the old copy
  }
  ScriptProperties.setProperty('docCopyId', docCopyId);// and store
the id of the new one
```

We store the ID of the copy so we can delete it when we don't need it anymore (that is, on the next run) using `ScriptProperties`, just like we did earlier in the "Boss mail" example. The following code snippet depicts the replacement of the placeholders:

```
var copy = DocumentApp.openById(docCopyId);
copy.getBody().replaceText('#day#', headers[todayInSheet]);
for(var n=0 ; n<menuTitle.length-1 ; n++){ // loop every item except
image URL
  copy.getBody().replaceText('#'+menuTitle[n]+'#',menuData[n]);
}
var image = DriveApp.getFileById(menuData[n].split('d/')[1].
split('/')[0]).getBlob();// retrieve ID from URL
var imagePlace = copy.getBody().findText('#'+menuTitle[n]+'#').
getElement().getParent();
  imagePlace.asParagraph().appendInlineImage(image).setWidth(300).
setHeight(200);
  imagePlace.asText().deleteText(0, 22);
```

We replace all the placeholders we have in our master document. As you can notice, we use #name# to mark the placeholders. DocumentApp has a very convenient method especially designed for that purpose. The following line of code shows the method used to save and close the document:

```
copy.saveAndClose();
```

We need to make sure that every change is made as expected and the document gets updated.

```
var htmlContent = "<table class='sites-layout-name-one-column sites-
layout-hbox' cellspacing='0'><tbody><tr><td class='sites-layout-
tile sites-tile-name-content-1'><div dir='ltr'><div/><div><div
class='sites-embed-align-left-wrapping-off'><div style='width:100%;'
class='sites-embed-border-on sites-embed sites-embed-full-width'><h4
class='sites-embed-title'> </h4><div style='display:none;'
class='sites-embed-object-title'> </div><div class='sites-embed-
content sites-embed-type-writely'><iframe frameborder='0' title=' '
height='900' width='100%' src='http://docs.google.com/document/previe
w?hgd=1&amp;id="+docCopyId+"'/></div></div></div></div><hr/></div></
td></tr></tbody></table>"
```

The preceding lines of code are a bit tricky. We have copied the HTML content of our web page that has an embedded document in a frame, and we simply replaced the fixed document ID with the variable docCopyId, which is the ID of the document we just created. The site page will display this document and render it perfectly. It is, I admit, a workaround I use because there is no getContentAsHtml method available yet in DocumentApp (nor in DriveApp). The following piece of code shows methods for calling the site object:

```
//  var site = SitesApp.getActiveSite();
  var site = SitesApp.getSite('privategasexperiments');
```

Here, we have to choose either of the preceding methods; if we have embedded the HTML code on our site, we can use getActiveSite(). If we have attached it to the document or the spreadsheet, we have to get the site by its name. Both methods will return a site object.

```
var oldPage = site.getChildByName('menuoftheday')
  if(oldPage!=null){oldPage.deletePage()};
```

In the preceding code, we check if the page exists before deleting it. If we didn't check, we might get an exception when trying to delete a page that doesn't exist.

And finally, in the following code, recreate the new page with the new content straight from the HTML string we built previously.

```
var newPage = site.createWebPage('Menu of the day', 'menuoftheday',
htmlContent);
}
```

And that's it! You need to create a clock trigger that will execute the updateSite() function every day after midnight (and preferably after your restaurant has closed for the day) so that your site page is always up to date without any effort.

To change the menu, edit the spreadsheet's contents and add new meals. You can always run it manually as often as you like to see the result online.

We could have created that trigger in the script as we did for the other examples, but let us keep it as simple as possible. This trigger needs to be set just once—that's not too much work I guess.

The documents I used in the previous example are available as templates. Make your own copy to be able to change their contents.

The spreadsheet can be found at the following link:

```
https://docs.google.com/spreadsheets/d/1Sa9Mah6eFbjZBEq5t0GtyMo_
NjHZfnJ-SXwW409xUD8/edit?usp=sharing
```

The document template can be found at the following link:

```
https://docs.google.com/document/d/1f4uW-Ol3xsmQspsseipDcHIw_
mUC1kpEQ6Js7rhFUxk/edit?usp=sharing
```

The following screenshot shows the spreadsheet:

	A	B	C	D	E	F	G	H
1		Monday	Tuesday	Wednesday	Thursday	Friday	Saturday	Sunday
2	starter	Miniature Yorkshire Pudd	Gourmet Pork, Prune an	Roast Tomato and Basil	Chicken Liver Pâté with	Norfolk Dressed Crab	Herb Breaded Mushroom	Warm Scotch Egg
3	main course	German lemon salmon	Belgian fried chicken	Pork stew with lentils	Famous "Coq au vin"	Seared baby calamary,to	Roasted baby lamb, juic	Mince Beef, Onion, Pea
4	dessert	Black chocolate mousse	Chestnut "millefeuille"	Marinated cherries in sch	Assortment of cheese	Berthillon mandarina sor	Tiramisu with mixed berr	Blackberry, Apple and H
5	image	I/0B3qSFd3iikE3UmpjelR	0B3qSFd3iikE3N2ZWSz2	I/0B3qSFd3iikE3UmpjelR	0B3qSFd3iikE3N2ZWSz2	I/0B3qSFd3iikE3UmpjelR	0B3qSFd3iikE3N2ZWSz2	I/0B3qSFd3iikE3UmpjelR

The following screenshot shows the template:

The following screenshot shows the site's page on a Thursday:

Creating pages

The previous example actually doesn't have many SiteApp service methods as it again makes use of a combination of sites, documents, and spreadsheets, which is one of the major interests of the Google platform. Google services are always available and tend to exchange data to and from each other (https://developers.google.com/apps-script/reference/sites).

We could have got almost the same result using a different approach and using only SiteApp methods.

In that workflow, we'll need to create a second website with restricted access rights in which we are going to create seven pages, one for each day of the week, with a menu description on each page.

In this case, we could have a different layout for each day, such as varying font styles and background images.

From there on, the only thing we have to do is copy the appropriate page to our public website every day, just like we did in the first example.

This can easily be achieved using the template feature in SiteApp. Each page will be published as a template on your private site, and this template will be used to create new pages on your public site.

The code is pretty short and is as follows:

```
// this script will be embedded in your public site
   so it is the active one
// change this global variable to yours
var privateSite = SitesApp.getSite('myPrivateSiteName');

function updateSite() {
  var today = new Date().getDay();// in JS Sunday is 0
  var pageNames =
['sunday','monday','tuesday','wednesday','thursday','friday',
'saturday'];// the page names in an array
  var site = SitesApp.getActiveSite();
  var pageToUse = privateSite.getChildByName
(pageNames[today]+'_template')
  if(pageToUse == null){ // if the page is not a template yet
    pageToUse = privateSite.getChildByName(pageNames[today]).
publishAsTemplate(pageNames[today]+'_template'); //
then make it a template
```

```
    privateSite.getChildByName(pageNames[today]).
setName(pageNames[today]+'_draft');// and save the draft
with a new name
    }
    var oldPage = site.getChildByName('menuoftheday')
    if(oldPage!=null){oldPage.deletePage()};// delete the current
page after checking it exists
    var newPage = site.createPageFromTemplate('Menu for
'+pageNames[today], 'menuoftheday', pageNames[today]+'_template');//
and create the page with the right name and title from the template
    }
```

The preceding code is really straightforward and includes comments that explain what we do in every step.

I'm not sure which approach is better. The only thing I can say is that I like to use different methods from different Google Apps Script services and make them work together, so I prefer the first approach; but, I'd agree that it's not a valid motivation.

Interactivity

The example shown here can be viewed online. A form can be filled in, and the site's user list will be updated. Feel free to have a look at the following link:

```
https://sites.google.com/site/gettingstartedwithgas/home
```

Different sources of data can be used to automatically update Google Sites as follows:

- **Forms**: These can be embedded, and their responses can be used to create or modify pages
- **Calendars**: These can be embedded, and it's easy to retrieve data from them to update a page
- **Spreadsheets**: These can be published to web pages, but when they are published, they don't work as spreadsheets anymore and are just visible as pages; if you have edit rights, you will be able to see a link to open them in the normal spreadsheet interface
- **Text documents**: The same comments apply to text documents, as we saw in our example of the restaurant menu
- **Script gadgets**: These can be embedded as well, and from there on, you will be able to perform any data manipulation and site update possible

Another feature that we haven't mentioned yet is the ability of Google Sites to change the sharing settings using a script.

A typical use case would be to automate edit access to a site after a user submits a form so that the user can post messages after logging in.

Let us try a simplified version of such a workflow that doesn't actually change the access right because it doesn't ask for an e-mail address (it's just a test!) but uses the same workflow and just displays a list, such as a list of names (or pseudo) and comments, on the site's page.

To make it a real logging site, you just have to ask for an e-mail and use that e-mail to add an editor to the site. You could even simply add a function that removes all the editors after some time so that access gets granted only for the current day.

The following script contains a few interesting elements that we can use in many other cases. I'll explain it step-by-step.

```
functionfunctionGrantAccess(eventInfo) {
    Logger.log(JSON.stringify(eventInfo));
```

The preceding code is used to see the content of eventInfo, which is the event that gets triggered on form submission. Looking at the logger will show us how it is actually built. We'll need it a little later.

```
var time = eventInfo.namedValues['Timestamp'];
var userName = eventInfo.namedValues['user name'];
var comment = eventInfo.namedValues['a comment];
```

The preceding three lines retrieve values from the eventInfo object as documented at https://developers.google.com/apps-script/understanding_events.

```
var site = SitesApp.getSite('gettingstartedwithgas');
var userPage = site.getChildByName('login/users');
```

The preceding lines of code depict the site objects, which are the site and the page we want to write to.

```
var logUsers = 'Logged Users list :<br><br>';
```

The previous line of code depicts the logUsers variable that we shall fill with the user list to publish it on the page;
 is the HTML tag that has been used to create a "new line".

```
var sheet = SpreadsheetApp.getActive().getSheetByName('Form
Responses 2');
var data = sheet.getDataRange().getValues();// get data from sheet
var headers = data.shift();
```

We already used the preceding code to get data from the spreadsheet and get the header out of the array.

```
data.sort(function(x,y){// adding a function to sort
var xp = x[1]; // allows to sort on column B
var yp = y[1];
return xp == yp ? 0 : xp<yp ? -1 : 1;// sort 'ascending'
  });
```

The preceding code is new and interesting. I wanted to sort the array on the second column because the first column is a timestamp and I didn't care about the time of form submission.

The sort() method has an optional function that returns 0, +1, or -1 depending on the order of xp and yp, and the sorting follows that rule. In this case, we take xp=x[1], which is the second column in the array (and in the sheet), and sort it in ascending order (replace < with > to get the descending order).

```
var unique = [];// create new array to store data without duplicates
unique.push(data[0]);// keep the first item
for(var n=1 ; n<data.length ; n++){ // loop through data
  if(data[n][1]+data[n][2] != data[n-1][1]+data[n-1][2]){
    unique.push(data[n]);// if different from previous then keep
  }
}
```

With the preceding loop, we skip any duplicates in the list. It works because the data has been sorted and it doesn't care about column 1 in the spreadsheet, so a timestamp is not part of the comparison.

```
unique.unshift(headers);// add the header back on top of the array
for(var n=0 ; n<unique.length ; n++){
  Logger.log(unique[n]);// just to check more easily the sorting and
duplicate remove
  logUsers+='<br>'+unique[n].join('  -  ');
  }
```

Build the output string with separators (and   ) and <br> tags as shown in the preceding code.

```
userPage.setHtmlContent(logUsers);
```

Write the logUser HTML string to the site page using the preceding line of code.

```
sheet.getDataRange().clear();// clear the sheet
sheet.getRange(1,1,unique.length, unique[0].length).
setValues(unique);// and write the new values
}
```

After this, renew the values in the spreadsheet with the preceding code. To make it simple, we just wipe everything out and write it back.

Now, this function has to be triggered on form submission. We have already seen how to set up a trigger. Now we need to navigate to **Resources | Current script triggers | add a new trigger** and choose **on form submit** for that function. This is simple, but it means that the function can only be tested on submitting forms, which is annoying and time consuming, so let us see how we can work around that.

Using the logger service and the `JSON.stringify(eventInfo)` method, we can see how this `eventInfo` object looks; a typical example is as follows:

```
/* {"namedValues":{"user name":["test name"],"a comment":["gxfgxdfhdgf
hjfgjhfgjxfgj"],"Timestamp":["1/2/2014 22:17:24"]},"values":["1/2/2014
22:17:24","test name","gxfgxdfhdgfhjfgjhfgjxfgj"],"source":{},"range":
{"rowStart":2,"rowEnd":2,"columnEnd":3,"columnStart":1}}
*/
```

The braces mean that `namedValues` is a JavaScript object (we knew that already!), but the first property of this object has only one value that also starts with a brace. This means that it is also an object.

And the second object has the properties that interest us, `user name` and `a comment`, exactly how we created them in the form. It also has parameters for `range` and `Timestamp`.

With this knowledge, we can now build new objects with all the necessary properties and use them to test our function. The object `eventInfo` has only one property (`namedValues`) and its value, and the second object `namedValues` has our useful properties.

The code to create the "fake form answer" and also call our main function is as follows:

```
function testGrantAccess() {
var eventInfo = {};
var namedValues = {};  namedValues['Timestamp'] = '2010/03/12 15:00';
  namedValues['user name'] = 'bob smith';
  namedValues['a comment'] = 'Bla'Blablabla...';
  eventInfo['namedValues'] = namedValues
  GrantAccess(eventInfo);
}
```

The result of the preceding code is just the same as submitting a form. Magic, isn't it?

This code is embedded in a shared spreadsheet; it can be found at the following link:

```
https://docs.google.com/spreadsheets/d/10aKXGDxwCW6mDbp5ruIwpKXgRx3Hh
ibga4moghDxK3o/edit?usp=sharing
```

The following screenshot displays the page that was created:

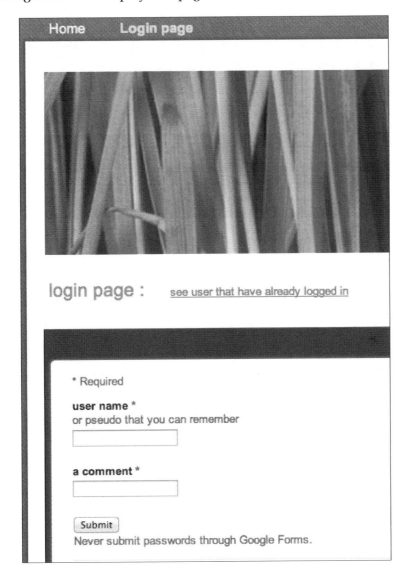

Summary

Although this chapter was meant to be about Google sites, it actually demonstrates the multiple features and advantages of the communication and combination of multiple services provided by Google Apps Script.

A Google site on its own is not very different from other sites. In many aspects, it is limited in layout compared to other platforms. However, its ability to integrate scripts and exchange data with every other Google service makes it a lot more interesting.

We have also had the opportunity to use a few interesting JavaScript features that we will surely use multiple times, and it is definitely motivating that we have a chance to get our hands on the user interface tools in the next chapter.

6
Standalone Web Applications / User Interfaces

It is sometimes useful to write standalone web applications that can be shared across offices or with other users; these applications would need an intuitive user interface. This chapter will teach you how to build these interfaces.

If you are a Google Docs user (and if you read this book, you certainly will be), you probably like the ability to share documents with friends or co-workers, but you would sometimes like the option to not share every part of it.

For example, it would be nice for one to be able to see data about themselves on a spreadsheet, but not all the data about everyone. As we experienced before, spreadsheets, for example, can be selectively write-protected, but there is no way to hide ranges selectively depending on the user viewing it.

We could imagine some workaround by copying part of the sheet to a new one and sharing this one, but then we'd have to take care to synchronize these sheets. When we have many people to share with, this might quickly become very complicated.

This situation is a good example for showing how designing a dedicated user interface can be an elegant solution, but we shall see that there are many others too.

UI or not UI, that's the question

Spreadsheets and text documents are by nature very powerful and well-designed interfaces; they are the result of many years of expertise from Google and other previous designs as well, but for some use cases there are just too many possibilities.

If you have already found one of your cherished and carefully prepared documents completely messed up by someone after you gave them access to it, you'll understand what I mean.

It is not always a question of malice or wickedness but, very often, a simple matter of incompetence.

Building a user interface with restricted possibilities solves that problem radically; it just requires a little more work from our side and that's what we're going to try now.

This chapter is about standalone web apps and UIs; we'll see that there are also many situations in which we don't need a user interface and others in which applications respond to parameters or even work entirely on their own without any user interaction.

Common concepts to all web apps

Any application that we use in our computer environment has a name and, for local computer programs, a container with an extension (`.app`, `.exe`, `.com`, and so on), but web apps don't: they generally have an address corresponding to a web page somewhere and when the page is loaded, the application starts executing.

Google web applications work this way, but remember that the code we write does not run on the user's computer but on Google's server. This workflow will have an effect on the speed of our apps: before showing a single pixel on our screen, the server has to execute most of the code and this can take a while in some cases. I have written some scripts that just don't work for some users because they have simply too much data on their drive and it's taken more than 5 minutes to prepare this data for display. I'll try to avoid such examples here so that you don't lose time on them, but we should keep this speed aspect in mind at all times and try to be as efficient as we can.

Some parts of the code we are going to use in web apps are executed differently; the code is served to our browser and executed in the browser itself, meaning that the execution speed depends only on the speeds of the browser JavaScript engine and our processor, which in both cases are far superior to what can be expected from the combination of Google server speed, transfer speed, and Internet speed we use in normal scripts.

This so-called client-side code support is a relatively new feature introduced with HtmlService (it is already present in a few methods of UiApp, but only for minor details) and opens new perspectives for a lot of applications as we'll see in the *Building an amazing UI* section.

Note that a client-side JavaScript is more browser dependent than a server-side apps script and that some JavaScript methods could return different results on different browsers, particularly regarding CSS styling. See the Google recommendations on this subject at `https://support.google.com/drive/answer/2375082?hl=en`.

One last important aspect of code writing for standalone web apps is the entry point of the script. The execution has to start at one point: as I mentioned earlier, a normal JavaScript starts when the page loads—that's simple and logical—but the script we write for a Google web app can't work this way. The server doesn't know what we do when it receives the code; it must compile the script to serve a user interface and only then can we interact with it.

Considering all this, we have to define a starting point: a function that will be executed in the very first place and served back to our browser that is waiting for us to do something; this function has a standard name: `doGet()`.

Every web app in Google Apps Script will begin with `doGet()` and generally create the UI in that `doGet` function (but that is not mandatory).

Building an efficient UI

Let us start with something simple that we'll examine in full detail, for example, the code we used in the previous chapter to calculate the hours since our birth date and time (again!).

The online Google's documentation also explains in detail how this works (`https://developers.google.com/apps-script/guides/ui-service`).

In this example, we use UiApp, which was the first user interface design service offered by Google Apps Script and is based on **Google Web Toolkit (GWT)**, an open source project developed by Google and used in many other projects (`https://developers.google.com/apps-script/reference/ui`).

The documentation explains that it might be useful to read the GWT doc as well, but I'm afraid that is far beyond the scope of this book and too much information to digest for a typical user. I personally consider the UiService documentation sufficient enough to use even for complex projects.

Note that the UiService is marked as experimental, which means that Google does not guarantee its sustainability over time; but, for now they don't seem to be abandoning it.

After this preliminary information, let's have a look at how it works:

```
function doGet() {
```

The entry point of every web app is a function called `doGet`, as mentioned earlier in this chapter. This tells the server that it must start executing the script right there. What follows can be using UiService, or HtmlService, or even ContentService; in every case, it's all about scripts that create apps that are not bounded to any type of document and work on their own. All three services are documented in the script part of the reference documentation (`https://developers.google.com/apps-script/reference/ui/`, `https://developers.google.com/apps-script/reference/html/`, and `https://developers.google.com/apps-script/reference/content/`).

The following code can be used for building a UI:

```
var app = UiApp.createApplication().setTitle('Age In Hours');
```

The variable `app` that we create represents an instance of the UI.

This concept is important because it means that if more than one user calls that function simultaneously, there will be those many instances of this project and each of them will be completely independent. It also means that once we create that instance, we must always refer to it in any other parts of the script or any other functions in which it is used. We'll refer to it using a `getActiveApplication()` statement. We also gave a title to the app; this is the name that will appear at the top of the browser window. The following line of code will create a grid in our UI:

```
var grid = app.createGrid(3,2);
```

This is the first object we create in our UI; it is a grid composed of three rows and two columns. The following code shows the second most important concept of UiApp—the handler:

```
var handler =
    app.createServerHandler('myAgeInHours').addCallbackElement(grid);
```

A handler is a description of what should happen when the user does something. "Something" means any phenomena, such as `keypress`, `mouseover`, and `hover`, that are detected by the browser as events. Handlers are normally written for these events. They are nothing but functions, which are invoked whenever such an event occurs. It is one of the core concepts of how event-driven asynchronous programming is designed.

Right after this method, we find the `addCallbackElement()` statement that tells the handler what data must be sent to the `handler` function.

This data is again a JavaScript object that can be a single widget (a widget is a UI element) or as in this example, a container for many widgets. It is a good practice to choose the highest-level container as the call-back element to make things easier, but one could also add every necessary widget one by one. It's just good manners to eventually forget one!

```
var time = app.createListBox().setName('time').addItem('Choose the
hour',-1);

for(var n=0 ; n<24 ; n++){time.addItem(n+' h',n)};
```

This is the first widget that will be placed in the grid: a simple `listBox` in which we add a few items. See the documentation (`https://developers.google.com/apps-script/reference/ui/list-box`) for details about how it can be used. We have added text to indicate what to do and in the following code, we add 24 hours to choose from. (Note that we add two values in each item: one is the shown value (a string) and the other is the returned value (in this case, a number).)

```
var date = app.createDateBox().setName('date');
var button = app.createButton('Show me...',handler);
grid.setWidget(0,0,date).setWidget(0,1,time).setWidget(1,0,button);
app.add(grid);
```

Then we add a few other widgets, such as `dateBox` to enter a date and a button to trigger the handler, and place all of them on the grid. We then add the grid to the UiApp instance; finally, we must tell the UiApp instance to return that onscreen. To do that, we use the following line of code:

```
return app;
}
```

This function is now closed with a closing brace and can be tested as it is.

This step needs a little more explanation because if you simply run that function, you won't get any error but neither will anything happen!

As I already mentioned in a previous chapter, web apps have to be published before they can be used, but some time ago, Google introduced a second step that allows users to have two URLs for every application.

The first URL is a development version that corresponds to the script you just saved and the second one corresponds to a specific version of the script that you can save separately.

This allows us to work on a script in the development version and when it is sufficiently stable, create a version that can be shared with anyone. Any change made to the script afterwards will not be reflected in the shared version until we update it to a new version.

Both URLs are shown in the deployment pop-up screen; the shareable one is shown as a URL, while the development URL is only available as a link, as illustrated in the following screenshot:

The development URL version can easily be saved from the **File** menu; you can create as many versions as you need as shown in the following screenshot:

Once you have saved the first version of your script, you can deploy it
(menu bar | **Publish** | **Deploy as web app**) and use the development URL
to see whether or not your script works as expected.

The following screenshot shows what you should get in a new browser tab
(or window):

In the browser tab shown in the previous screenshot, you can select a date (or type a
date) in the first box and choose an hour in the drop-down list.

You can even click on the **Show me...** button, but you will get an error message
telling you: **Error encountered: Script function not found: myAgeInHours**, which is
the logical action of the handler we created in the doGet function; it calls the function
named myAgeInHours and does not find it.

So let us write the code as follows:

```
function myAgeInHours(e){
var app = UiApp.getActiveApplication();
```

As we saw earlier, there is one instance of the app variable and we have to get it to
communicate with it. That's the purpose of the statement getActiveApplication().

Also note that our function has a parameter named e, which is the object that has all
the information from the doGet function, that is, the content of the callBackElement
parameter we added, the origin of the trigger, and a few others. The following lines
of code give the returned value for date in milliseconds and the returned value in
hours, combined with a condition:

```
var myBirthDate = e.parameter.date.getTime();// the returned value
   for date (in milliseconds)
var time = Number(e.parameter.time) == - 1 ? 0 :
   Number(e.parameter.time);// the returned value in hours combined
   with a condition
```

One of the properties of the e object is called parameter and has the keys and values
that we are looking for; the values in the dateBox class and the value from the list,
both are represented by their names as defined in the doGet function.

Another important point is that the name of the widget is used as a key parameter to retrieve its value. We'll see that we can also define an ID for any widget if we want to modify its value or do anything with it.

So, `e.parameter.time` returns the value that was selected in the `listBox` class named `time`; this value is a number, but when we get it back, it has become a string representation of the number (which, in fact, you don't see because they look exactly the same, of course); therefore, we used the `Number(e.parameter.time)` function to make it a number again.

`Number()` is a standard JavaScript function documented at `https://developer. mozilla.org/en-US/docs/Web/JavaScript/Reference/Global_Objects/Number`.

Following is the complete content of the event info object (`e`), shown in the logger using the `JSON.stringify()` utility function we already used:

```
{"parameter":{"clientY":"119","clientX":"158","eventType":"click","da
te":"2014-01-05T23:00:00.000Z","ctrl":"false","meta":"false","time":"1
0","source":"u331805504378","button":"1","alt":"false","screenY":"236"
,"screenX":"316","y":"35","shift":"false","x":"101"}}
```

We can see that the object is built almost exactly the same way as it was in the form service we examined in the previous chapter: the `parameter` key has an object as value and this object has a number of properties among which we find our widgets' names, the source of the event, the current position of the cursor in the UI (x and y) and on the screen (screenX and screenY), and flags describing the keyboard use (*Alt* and *Shift*). If you remember how we built the form service example, you will easily understand why we use a two-level method to retrieve the values: `parameter` for the first level and `name` for the second level.

Just about every value returned by this `e.parameter` mechanism returns a string representation; there is one exception though: dates are returned as JavaScript date objects. No luck—we used a date in our first example!

The next part of the code, shown as follows, has nothing new compared to the former version; it comprises only a couple of math operations:

```
myBirthDate = parseInt(myBirthDate/3600000, 10);
var today = parseInt(new Date().getTime()/3600000, 10);
```

But, the end is again specific to the web app context; we are creating a new widget (a label) to show the result of our math operations as follows:

```
app.add(app.createLabel().setText('there are '+(today-myBirthDate-
time)+' hours between now and your birth date !'));// write the result
in a 'label'
return app; // this tells the script to update the Ui
}
```

Using the instance of the UI that we retrieved in the `app` variable (`UiApp.getActiveApplication();`), we can create a widget the same way we did in the `doGet` function and add it to the `app` variable.

Then we return the `app` variable to tell the script to actually show the result and update the browser.

Now we can save the script and go back to our development URL tab, eventually refreshing the browser and trying again.

When we fill both fields and click on the **Show me...** button, the result shows up right under the button.

This was our first example from start to end with all the details.

It does indeed work, but we have to admit it looks ugly!

Building a good-looking UI

UiService offers a lot of possibilities to improve the design of web apps; there's the possibility of using the numerous CSS arguments to customize elements (also visit the Wikipedia page about CSS at `http://en.wikipedia.org/wiki/CSS`).

The main difference is that we don't use style sheets but add a style to each widget individually in the code itself.

We have the following two methods to set a style:

- The `setStyleAttribute(name,value)` method accepts a single pair of parameters (`https://developers.google.com/apps-script/reference/ui/button#setStyleAttribute(String,String)`).

- The `setStyleAttributes({objects with name/attributes parameters pairs})` method takes objects as parameters. (`https://developers.google.com/apps-script/reference/ui/button#setStyleAttributes(Object)`). The list of all the available attributes currently supported in UiApp is documented at `https://developers.google.com/apps-script/ui_supportedStyles`.

The first method in the bullet list is useful for a single parameter, but we often prefer the second one because it allows for a more compact and easy-to-read code.

Our previous code could be improved with a few CSS attributes, for example, adding a `padding` value could keep the widgets distant from the window's border and `background` could color the background of our app. The button could have a different size and rounded borders. The following is the modified code and its onscreen result:

```
function doGet() {
    var app = UiApp.createApplication().setTitle('Age In Hours');
    var grid = app.createGrid(3,2).setStyleAttributes({'padding':'50px',
'background':'#FFA'});
    var handler = app.createServerHandler('myAgeInHours').
addCallbackElement(grid);
    var time = app.createListBox().setName('time').addItem('Choose the
hour',-1);
    for(var n=0 ; n<24 ; n++){time.addItem(n+' h',n)};
    var date = app.createDateBox().setName('date');
    var button = app.createButton('Show me...',handler).setStyleAttribut
es({'padding':'15px', 'border-radius':'10px', 'borderWidth':'5px', 'bo
rderColor':'#DDD','fontSize':'16pt'});
    grid.setWidget(0,0,date).setWidget(0,1,time).setWidget(1,0,button);
    app.add(grid);
    return app;
}
```

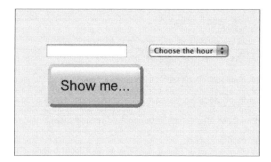

As you'll probably notice, setting the attributes for every widget in the script rapidly takes up a lot of space in the code; to avoid that, we can define style objects outside of the function as global variables (global variables in Google Apps Script can only be constants, as we have seen in *Chapter 1, Enhancing Spreadsheets*) and assign their properties to each widget in a more simple and compact way.

It would simply be like the following code:

```
var styleGrid = {'padding':'50px', 'background':'#FFA'};
var styleButton = {'padding':'15px', 'border-radius':'10px',
    'borderWidth':'5px', 'borderColor':'#DDD','fontSize':'16pt'};
```

```
function doGet() {
  var app = UiApp.createApplication().setTitle('Age In Hours');
  var grid = app.createGrid(3,2).setStyleAttributes(styleGrid);
  var handler = app.createServerHandler('myAgeInHours').
addCallbackElement(grid);
  var time = app.createListBox().setName('time').addItem('Choose the
hour',-1);
  for(var n=0 ; n<24 ; n++){time.addItem(n+' h',n)};
  var date = app.createDateBox().setName('date');
  var button = app.createButton('Show me...',handler).setStyleAttribut
es(styleButton);
  grid.setWidget(0,0,date).setWidget(0,1,time).setWidget(1,0,button);
  app.add(grid);
  return app;
}
```

The previous code returns exactly the same result. Note that the script editor doesn't set colors to global variable names defined outside of any function, but accepts this method without posing any issues. When building complex UIs, this method is much simple to use and can almost be considered as an equivalent to using CSS like one does in normal HTML page design.

We can even create a new script file within the project (**File** | **New** | **Script file**) to hold all the style variable definitions to help keep our script tidy and clean.

Now that we have a handle on the basics of UiApps, let's try a more useful example with a slightly more complex (and hopefully better looking) UI.

The following application was designed to allow people in the school I work for to subscribe to some of the numerous calendars we have. Actually, each class, each classroom, and each group of teachers has their own calendar; in other words, about everything has a calendar, which makes it really tedious to manually subscribe to each of them using the sharing URLs, so the following application was really welcomed when I wrote it:

```
The code can be divided in eight functions and, of course, the one
that creates the user interface is called doGet!
//---------------------------------------------------------------
//  Global variable
//---------------------------------------------------------------
  var email = String(Session.getUser().getUserLoginId());
  //
```

This web app runs as the user accessing the application, which means that we can get the e-mail address of its user and have access to their calendars. If this weren't the case, it would become completely useless. The code for the calendar example is as follows:

```
function doGet(){
  var app =
    UiApp.createApplication().setHeight(400).setWidth(650).
setStyleAttribute('background', 'beige').setTitle("Group calendar
manager");
  var panel =
    app.createAbsolutePanel().setStyleAttribute('padding', '25');
  var Vpanel = app.createVerticalPanel();
  var grid = app.createGrid(6, 2).setWidth('550').setId('grid');
  var Slist=
    app.createListBox(true).setName("slb").setId("slb").
setVisibleItemCount(16).setWidth("180").setStyleAttribute('margin-
left', '5px');
  var Ulist=
    app.createListBox(true).setName("ulb").setId("ulb").
setVisibleItemCount(16).setWidth("195").setStyleAttribute('margin-
left', '5px');
  var subs =
    app.createButton("Subscribe to selected calendars").
setWidth("180");
  var unsubs = app.createButton("Unsubscribe from selected
calendars").setWidth("195");
  var quit = app.createButton("Quit (and delete any personal data from
this application)");
  var avert = app.createLabel("Only group calendar are listed
    here, your personal calendar won't appear",true).setWidth('250');
  var comment = app.createLabel("You can select more that one
    calendar at a time",true).setWidth('250');
  var wait = app.createLabel("****  PLEASE WAIT
    ****",true).setWidth('250').setStyleAttribute('borderWidth',
    '2').setStyleAttribute('background','yellow').setId('wait').
setVisible(false);
  var ok = app.createLabel("Your calendars have been updated.
    Allow a couple of seconds before
    checking",true).setWidth('250').setVisible(false).setId('ok');
  var log = app.createLabel("You are connected as
    "+email,true).setWidth('250').setStyleAttribute('background','w
hite').setStyleAttribute('padding', '8').setStyleAttribute('margin-
left', '5px');
  var end = app.createHTML("<BR><BR>Thanks for using this
    application, you may close this window<BR><BR><BR>© serge
    2014").setId('end').setVisible(false);
```

```
      var anchor = app.createAnchor('to calendar page',
   'https://www.google.com/calendar');
      grid.setWidget(0, 0, Slist)
           .setWidget(0, 1, Ulist)
           .setWidget(1, 0, subs)
           .setWidget(1, 1, unsubs)
           .setWidget(2, 1, avert)
           .setWidget(2, 0, comment)
           .setWidget(3, 0, wait)
           .setWidget(4, 0, log)
           .setWidget(5, 0, quit)
           .setWidget(4, 1, anchor)
           .setWidget(5, 1, ok);// place all widgets on the grid
      Vpanel.add(grid).add(end);
      app.add(panel.add(Vpanel));
      updateLists(Slist,Ulist);//
         call the function to populate the lists
      var handlerSub =
         app.createServerHandler("calsub").addCallbackElement(grid);
           subs.addClickHandler(handlerSub);
      var handlerUnsub =
         app.createServerHandler("calunsub").addCallbackElement(grid);
           unsubs.addClickHandler(handlerUnsub);
      var handlerQuit =
         app.createServerHandler("quit").addCallbackElement(grid);
           quit.addClickHandler(handlerQuit);
      var cliHandlerSub = app.createClientHandler()
           .forTargets(wait).setVisible(true);
        subs.addClickHandler(cliHandlerSub);
      var cliHandlerUnsub = app.createClientHandler()
           .forTargets(wait).setVisible(true);
        unsubs.addClickHandler(cliHandlerUnsub);
      return app;
      }
```

There's nothing really new here, except that we used two different types of handlers: one that we tried already (ServerHandler) that tells the server which function to call and the other called clientHandler.

Let us look at it more closely and read the documentation about it (https://developers.google.com/apps-script/reference/ui/client-handler).

The following lines explain what the documentation says and verify what I explained before:

> *An event handler that runs in the user's browser without needing a call back to the server. These will, in general, run much faster than ServerHandlers but they are also more limited in what they can do.*

They can be used on just about any widget and one of their most current use cases is to show or enable another widget (and hide or disable it of course) because they are unable to execute any functions.

In the preceding example, it shows a yellow label saying PLEASE WAIT when a time-consuming process is started.

Practically, it means that both buttons in the UI have two clickHandler interfaces: one server handler that actually calls the function and a second that shows the message. As the second one works instantly, we can wait until the handler function finishes its task and returns an instruction to hide the message. The visual effect is exactly what we expected: the message is visible during the function execution.

Keep that idea at hand as you will most probably want to use it later.

Then come the different functions to get all the calendars, store them in a spreadsheet and then a database, and update the lists; there's even a special function to quit the application with a polite message. These functions are simply commented in the following code itself to briefly explain how they work:

```
function updateLists(Slist,Ulist){
  var app = UiApp.getActiveApplication();
  var db = ScriptDb.getMyDb();// create a Db instance
  var results = db.query({name: db.anyValue()}).sortBy("name",
    db.ASCENDING, db.LEXICAL);// get date from dB, sorted ascending
  var grouplist = [];
  while (results.hasNext()) {
    var item = results.next();
    Logger.log('item added to grouplist = '+item);
    grouplist.push([item.name,item.url]);
  }
  var emptyU = true;
  var emptyS = true;
  var Ulistvalid = [];// unsubscribe list
  var Slistvalid = [];// subscribe list
  var userlist = [];
  var Clist = CalendarApp.getAllCalendars();
  for(cc=0;cc<Clist.length;++cc){
```

```
      userlist.push(Clist[cc].getName());
      Logger.log('Clist[cc].getName() = '+Clist[cc].getName());
      if(grouplist.toString().match(Clist[cc].getName())
        ==Clist[cc].getName()){Ulistvalid.push([Clist[cc].
getName(),Clist[cc].getId()])}
    }
  Logger.log('Ulistvalid  = '+Ulistvalid);
  Logger.log('userlist  = '+userlist);
  for(cc=0;cc<Ulistvalid.length;++cc){
    Ulist.addItem(Ulistvalid[cc][0],Ulistvalid[cc][1]);
    emptyU = false;
  }
  for(cc=0;cc<grouplist.length;++cc){
    if(userlist.indexOf(grouplist[cc][0])==-1){
      Slist.addItem(grouplist[cc][0],grouplist[cc][1]);
      emptyS = false;
    }
  }
  if(emptyS){Slist.addItem('No Calendar available')};
  if(emptyU){Ulist.addItem('No calendar found')};
}
```

In the preceding function, we compare the calendars in the database to the user's ones. If the latter don't match any item in the database, we consider them private and don't show them. The following code explains the subscribe and unsubscribe processes for the calendar example:

```
function calsub(e){
  var app = UiApp.getActiveApplication();
  if(e.parameter.slb ==''){return};// if no calendar is selected
return immediately
  var Slist = app.getElementById('slb');
  var Ulist = app.getElementById('ulb');
  var ok = app.getElementById('ok').setText("Your calendars have been
updated. Allow a couple of seconds before checking");
  var calsubID = e.parameter.slb.split(',');// split the string to get
back an array
  Logger.log('calsubID = '+calsubID);
  for(nn=0;nn<calsubID.length;++nn){
    try{
      CalendarApp.subscribeToCalendar(calsubID[nn]);
    }catch(err){
      Logger.log(err)
      ok.setText("Error trying to get calendar, please retry - "+err);
      break;//if error exit loop
```

```
      }
    }
    Ulist.clear();
    Slist.clear();
    updateLists(Slist,Ulist);// updates the lists
    ok.setVisible(true);//show the confirmation or error message
    app.getElementById('wait').setVisible(false);// hide the wait
  message
    return app;//update Ui
  }


  function calunsub(e){
    var app = UiApp.getActiveApplication();
    if(e.parameter.ulb ==''){return};// if no calendar is selected
  return immediately
    var Slist = app.getElementById('slb');
    var Ulist = app.getElementById('ulb');
    var ok = app.getElementById('ok').setText("Your calendars have been
  updated. Allow a couple of seconds before checking");
    var calunsubID = e.parameter.ulb.split(',');// split the string to
  get back an array
    for (n=0;n<calunsubID.length;++n){
      Logger.log('calunsubID[n] = '+calunsubID[n]);
      try{
        CalendarApp.getCalendarById(calunsubID[n]).
  unsubscribeFromCalendar();
      }catch(err){
        Logger.log('ERROR message : '+err);
        ok.setText("Error trying to get calendar, please retry - "+err);
        break;//if error exit loop
      }
    }
    ok.setVisible(true);//show the confirmation or error message
    app.getElementById('wait').setVisible(false);// hide the wait
  message
    Ulist.clear();
    Slist.clear();
    updateLists(Slist,Ulist);// update lis(removed calendars are gone)
    return app;//update Ui
  }
```

The two functions `calsub(e)` and `calunsub(e)` take care of the actual subscribe and unsubscribe process. We use a `try/catch` structure to prevent execution when `calendarService` is not available (which happens sometimes) or when we're trying to unsubscribe to a calendar we own (see the documentation at `https://developers.google.com/apps-script/reference/calendar/calendar#unsubscribeFromCalendar()`).

```
function quit(){
    var app = UiApp.getActiveApplication();
    var grid = app.getElementById('grid').setVisible(false);
    var end = app.getElementById('end').setVisible(true);
    return app
}
```

The preceding code shows a **Goodbye** message when we close the application. Since there is no real way to actually close a Google Apps Script web app, we use this workaround to reassure the user that he will not be leaving his data exposed on the Internet. The following code will help us share the calendar using a spreadsheet:

```
function getlistFromSS(){
    var ss = SpreadsheetApp.getActiveSpreadsheet()
    var sh = ss.getSheets()[0];
    var last = ss.setActiveSheet(ss.getSheets()[0]).getLastRow();
    var list = sh.getRange(1,1,last,2).getValues();
    var key = [] ; var value = []
    deleteDb_()
    for(cc=0;cc<list.length;++cc){
      key.push(list[cc][0]);
      value.push(list[cc][1]);
    }
    for(cc=0;cc<key.length;++cc){
      var db = ScriptDb.getMyDb()
      db.save({name:key[cc], url:value[cc]})
      Logger.log(key[cc]+' --->  '+value[cc])
    }
}
```

You may now ask: why would we use a spreadsheet again? The only reason is that the calendar list has to be modified before we share this app (to remove any calendar we own and don't want to share) and a spreadsheet is the easiest way to handle that.

The web app part (the doGet function and its handlers) actually never reads that spreadsheet, so we don't have to share it with anybody. Even if someone finds a way to open this script and sees the spreadsheet ID, they won't be able to open it since it is private and I am the only person who can view and modify it. Data in ScriptDb (the database) is not protected but the data doesn't need to be hidden since the purpose of this script is to share these calendars. The following small function iterates the database and deletes every item in it:

```
function deleteDb_(){
  var db = ScriptDb.getMyDb();
  var results = db.query({name: db.anyValue()});
  while (results.hasNext()) {
    var item = results.next();
    db.remove(item);
  }
}
```

Note the underscore at the end of the function name; it prevents the function from appearing in the function list in the script editor. I used this feature because deleteDb_ is only called by another function in the script and never directly from the script editor menu. The following code has access to all the spreadsheets for the calendar example:

```
function getCallist(){
  var sh = SpreadsheetApp.getActiveSheet();
  var ss = SpreadsheetApp.getActiveSpreadsheet();
  var last = ss.getLastRow()==0 ? 1 : ss.getLastRow();
  sh.getRange(4, 1,last,2).clearContent();
  var list = new Array();
  list = CalendarApp.getAllCalendars()
  for (n=0;n<list.length;++n){
    var name = list[n].getName() ;
    var id = list[n].getId() ;
    sh.getRange(n+1,1).setValue(name)   ;
    sh.getRange(n+1,2).setValue(id)   ;
  }
}
```

The preceding function is the only function that has access to the spreadsheets; it gets all the user calendars and writes their names and IDs in two columns for visual control and editing, so you can remove the calendars you own and don't want to share.

The function is called from the script editor when we set up the application. This should seldom happen and only the script owner will be able to run it since the script file is not shared, nor is the spreadsheet. The following screenshot represents the data spreadsheet:

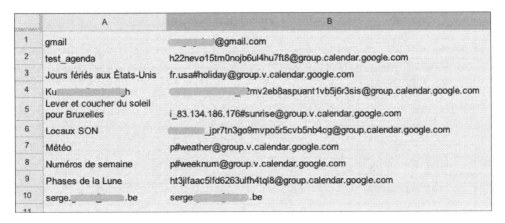

The following screenshot shows the final UI as the user will actually see it:

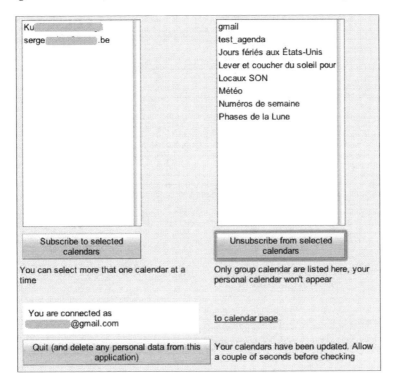

The last example shows how we can give many users access to spreadsheet data without showing the spreadsheet itself. The spreadsheet in our example was designed for an association that organizes a farm products buying group. They can send their orders every week for vegetables and other food products and they're all sent to the farmer every Thursday. The form is available Sunday through Wednesday and shows what products are available along with their prices.

The app also provides a separate link to a second UI for people to subscribe to and manage the distribution of their orders every week, with the ability to create events in their personal calendars.

The whole script is far too long to be published here, but it is available online in view mode for anyone with the link. You should make a copy of it if you intend to use it. The link is as follows:

```
https://docs.google.com/spreadsheet/ccc?key=0AnqSFd3iikE3dFBub2t1Ry1P
aXJUMUVkSVVSempCenc&usp=sharing
```

A public version of the app is also available without needing users to log in (`https://script.google.com/macros/s/AKfycbxr3GD8_ Vz9O3Rueqms6KzxYGc0yj33tynsxLJUZStjWVuE4ZAx/exec`); its functionality is reduced, so you can't obviously order anything for real, but every function works.

The following screenshot shows the planning calendar:

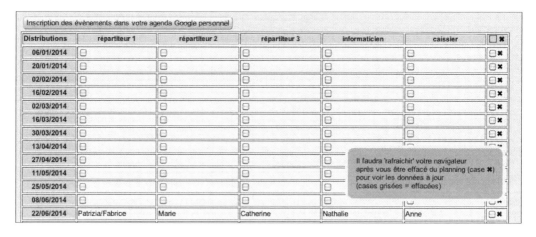

The following screenshot shows the actual order form:

Product	Origin	Unit	Price (€)	Quantité	Total	Remarque
Sauvegarde et calcul de la commande : total provisoire = 0,00 €				Accès direct au planning		
FRUITS						
Pineapple	Cameroun	PC	2,60 €	3		
Bananas	Rep Dominic	KG	2,40 €			
Lemon	Italy	250g	0,75 €	2		
Strawberry	Belgium	Box	4,20 €			
Kiwi	New Zealand	500g	1,95 €			
Melon	Spain	PC	2,40 €			
Orange	Italy	KG	6,50 €			
VEGETABLES						
Garlic	France	250g	2,95 €			
Artichoke	France	KG	3,00 €	2		
White asparagus	Ferme sainte Barbe	Bunch	8,00 €			
Eggplant	Holland	PC	4,00 €			
Avocado	Spain	PC	1,20 €			
Beetroot	Belgium	KG	2,60 €			
Broccoli	Belgium	KG	5,00 €	2		
Carrot	Ferme sainte Barbe	KG	1,00 €			
Purple carrot	Ferme sainte Barbe	PC	1,40 €			
Green celery	Belgium	PC	1,90 €			
Chervil	Belgium	PC	1,80 €	5		
White fungus	Holland	250g	1,65 €			
Button mushroom	Holland	250g	2,05 €			
Chinese cabbage	Belgium	PC	3,00 €			
Cauliflower	Belgium	PC	3,70 €			
Pointed head cabbage	Holland	PC	2,20 €			
Kohlrabi	Belgium	PC	1,60 €			
Cucumber	Belgium	KG	1,80 €			
Zucchini	Belgium	PC	3,00 €			
Cress	Holland	PC	2,10 €			
Cressonnette	Belgium	PC	1,00 €			
Spinach	Belgium	KG	4,50 €			
Fennel	Ferme sainte Barbe	KG	4,50 €			
Broad beans	France	KG	4,50 €			
Turnip	Belgium	KG	3,80 €			

These examples show that UiService allows for user interface building (at least IMHO) quite nicely, but we are limited to the available widgets and styles.

Another way to achieve even better results is using the HTML service.

Building an amazing UI

This section will show a single example that uses server code, JavaScript client code, and an external jQuery library.

We'll try to keep it as simple as possible, but you should know that there are probably no limits to what can be done with this toolset.

Your imagination and a few intentional limitations from Google will be the only limits. (`https://developers.google.com/apps-script/guides/html/restrictions/#adding_css_dynamically` and `https://developers.google.com/caja/docs/about/`).

I strongly recommend that before you try anything with HTML service, you take the time to read the documentation page about it (`https://developers.google.com/apps-script/guides/html/best-practices`) and have a look at the Caja page as well (`https://developers.google.com/caja/`).

Caja is a code compiler that is designed to sanitize JavaScript code, mainly to prevent from its misuse and any malware that JavaScript apps may contain.

In an introductory book such as this one, these concepts may seem a bit hard to understand. The example scripts presented are pretty basic and their purposes are clear and easy to comprehend, but you can easily imagine that a complex script can quickly become hard to read and very dangerous in terms of privacy or security.

Nevertheless, it is good to know that JavaScript is an evolved and powerful programming language that can do probably more than you imagine, both good and bad.

That's the idea behind the Caja project: make your JavaScript safe to use or embed it in your website by relying on an automatic code restriction process.

This peace of mind comes at a price: some scripts won't work and others may be too slow; but that's the choice Google made and I'm kind of happy they did.

If you find (and I would certainly understand if you did) that the Caja documentation is too complicated, don't worry too much; try your code and eventually test some parts on the Caja playground if you're unsure (`http://caja.appspot.com/`). Even if you don't clearly understand what's happening, you'll quickly learn enough to find your way through it.

The following code example uses the jQuery library for graphical features and shows you how to call a Google script function from a button that is defined in the HTML code itself.

It is built in four parts as follows:

- `code.gs`: It is a file that contains the GS code, including the `doGet()` function
- `demoCode.html`: It is the HTML code with the text and button definition
- `styleCSS.html`: It is the equivalent of a style sheet where all the `div` IDs are defined along with their formatting (color, opacity, position, and so on)
- `clientJavaScript`: It is the client JavaScript code

As explained in the documentation, the CSS file and client JavaScript file have to be explicitly included in the code; therefore, the line will be as follows:

```
function include(filename) {
  return
    HtmlService.createHtmlOutputFromFile(filename).getContent();
}
```

The code will tell the server to process those files along with the rendering of the page.

The following are the four code snippets; each of them will be pasted in different script files within a single project, using the name I've written as the first comment in each part:

```
//code.gs
function doGet() {
  return HtmlService.createTemplateFromFile('demoCode').evaluate().
setSandboxMode(HtmlService.SandboxMode.NATIVE);
}

function include(filename) {
  return HtmlService.createHtmlOutputFromFile(filename).getContent();
}

function sendEmail(){
  Logger.log('send email');
  MailApp.sendEmail(Session.getEffectiveUser().getEmail(),'A simple
message','... sent from yout html WebApp !\n\nI hope you like JQuery
animations.')
}
```

Then comes the HTML file as follows:

```
// html file
<?!= include('styleCSS'); ?>

<h2>Welcome to this demo,</h2>
```

```
<h1>Please use the below button to see what happens.<br><br>

<input type="button" value="Test button"
    onclick="google.script.run
        .withSuccessHandler(updateButton)
        .withUserObject(this)
        .sendEmail()" />
</h1>

<div id="tunnel"></div>
<div id="boule1"></div>
<div id="boule2"></div>
<div id="boule3"></div>
<h3>
Check your<br>email please...
</h3>
<h4>
Thanks for watching ;-)
</h4>

<?!= include('clientJavaScript'); ?>
```

Note that it is recommended that you place the JavaScript `include` at the end of the code, while the CSS, of course, comes at the beginning.

Then the CSS file that defines the graphic parameters of all the elements is as follows:

```
//styleCSS file<style>

#tunnel{
position:absolute;
top:250px;
background:#2bc1ce;
height:80px;
width:100%;
opacity:0;
}
#boule1{
position:absolute;
top:265px;
left:100px;
background:red;
opacity:0;
width:50px;
height:50px;
```

```
border-radius:50%
}

#boule2{
position:absolute;
top:265px;
left:200px;
background:blue;
opacity:0;
width:50px;
height:50px;
border-radius:50%
}

#boule3{
position:absolute;
top:265px;
left:300px;
background:green;
opacity:0;
width:50px;
height:50px;
border-radius:50%
}

h1{
padding-left : 20px;
font-family:Helvetica,Arial,sans-serif;
font-size:14pt;
color:#AAA;
}

h2{
padding : 20px;
font-family:Helvetica,Arial,sans-serif;
font-size:16pt;
color:#FFF;
background:#AAA;
}

h3{
position:absolute;
margin-left : 670px;
top:3000px;
```

```
font-family:Helvetica,Arial,sans-serif;
font-size:24pt;
color:white;
}

h4{
position:absolute;
margin-left : 580px;
top:400px;
font-family:Helvetica,Arial,sans-serif;
font-size:32pt;
color:blue;
opacity:0;
}

</style>
```

Finally, you can see the client JavaScript file that almost exclusively uses the jQuery functions in the following code:

```
// Client JavaScript file
<script>
  function updateButton(email, button) {
    button.value = 'Did you expect that ?';//update button text
    button.disabled = true;// disable button
$('#tunnel').animate({'opacity':1}, 2000);

// 1rst opacity balls
setTimeout(function(){
$('#boule1').animate({'opacity':.7},500);
},200);
setTimeout(function(){
$('#boule2').animate({'opacity':.7},1000);
},1200);
setTimeout(function(){
$('#boule3').animate({'opacity':.7},1500);
},2200);

// movement balls
setTimeout(function(){
$('#boule1').animate({'left':1300}, 4000).animate({'left':100},4000).
animate({'left':680},3000);
},3000);
setTimeout(function(){
```

```
$('#boule2').animate({'left':1000},4000).animate({'left':200},4000).
animate({'left':780},3000);
},3500);

setTimeout(function(){
$('#boule3').animate({'left':700},4000).animate({'left':1000},4000).
animate({'left':880},3000);
},4000);

// 2cnd opacity balls
setTimeout(function(){
$('#boule1').animate({'opacity':1},1000);
},4200);
setTimeout(function(){
$('#boule2').animate({'opacity':1},1000);
},4600);
setTimeout(function(){
$('#boule3').animate({'opacity':1},1000);
},5000);

// 3 balls are falling and get bigger
setTimeout(function(){
$('#boule1').animate({'top':2500, 'height':'800px', 'width':'800px'},
4000)
},7000);
setTimeout(function(){
$('#boule2').animate({'top':2500, 'height':'800px', 'width':'800px'},
4000)
},7300);
setTimeout(function(){
$('#boule3').animate({'top':2500, 'height':'800px', 'width':'800px'},
4000)
},7600);

// tunnel
setTimeout(function(){
$('#tunnel').animate({'width':'340px', 'height':'200px',
'left':'630'}, 4000)
},9000);

// text
setTimeout(function(){
$('h3').animate({'top':330},3000)
},12500);
```

```
//thanks
setTimeout(function(){
$('h4').animate({'opacity':.5},3000);
},15500);

}

</script>
```

After you have saved these four files and then saved and deployed a version for the project in exactly the same way we did for the other examples, you will get a URL that you can test.

If you are really curious, the following link is to an online dummy test that doesn't send any e-mails, but shows the UI exactly how it will be for your version:

```
https://script.google.com/macros/s/AKfycbzkF79ZLdw_Dgz7n6LcW0r7Lq53tI
uObifqH1903rf6kd-fPz8/exec
```

As you can see, the HTML service will set your creativity free of (almost) any limitations, but it is clearly a subject that could be covered in another book all by itself.

Limiting user access

Let us return for a while to publishing web apps, which we explored at the very beginning of this chapter: we saw that we could deploy them to run as **myself** and used by either **Anyone** or **only me**.

That's actually the first level of access limitation, but sometimes we would like to give access to some people we know and prevent everyone else from using it; this basic limitation is definitely too basic.

There are a few ways to get the result we want; the following are two simple examples.

When we deploy an app as **User accessing the web app**, the user will be asked to authorize the script to get his e-mail address (or more information if the app uses other Google services) and information about who is using it.

In this case, we can easily place a condition on this e-mail address for it to be compared to the list of authorized users. The following code for this is very simple:

```
var email = Session.getEffectiveUser().getEmail();
var client =
  ['serge@gmail.com','mary@yahoo.com','william@hotmail.com','jim@
gmail.com','xxx@gmail.com'];
```

Using the following code, we first create a list of valid e-mails in an array of strings and define a variable email, which is the e-mail address of the logged in user:

```
function doGet() {
  var app = UiApp.createApplication().setTitle('Checking user').
setStyleAttribute('background', '#DDD');
  var mainPanel = app.createVerticalPanel().setStyleAttribute('paddi
ng','25');
  var reject = app.createHTML("Hello,<BR><BR>You are connected
    with the user name <B>"+email+"</B> who is not authorized to
    use this app,<BR><BR>"+
                             "If you think this is an error please
contact the owner of this app at xxx@gmail.com<BR><BR>Thank you.").set
StyleAttribute('padding','25');
  for(n=0;n<client.length;++n){
    if(client[n].match(email)==email){
        var clientOK = true ; var name = client[n][0] ;
        break;
        };
  }
  if(!clientOK){
    app.add(reject);
    MailApp.sendEmail('scriptowner@gmail.com',
      'Someone with address ', email+' tried to connect without
authorization,
      think about calling him to chack what happened...');
    return app;
  }
  // here comes the normal code
  app.add(app.createLabel('Everything went right !!'));
  return app;
}
```

Then in the app, we set up a message to reject access for unauthorized users in a very polite way and compare the client e-mail with every item on our list. If the condition is true, we go on; otherwise, we show the rejection message and send ourselves an e-mail so we know something bad just happened (this is optional, of course). This option works only if people are asked to log in. In some cases, we would like it to work for anonymous access as well and we'll show that in our second example.

We can create special URLs with parameters that include user identification; the following is an example using `ContentService`, which offers a good opportunity to test that service as well:

```
function doGet(e) {
  var user = e.parameter.user;
  if(user!='giovanni'){return
    ContentService.createTextOutput("Logging error, you are not
authorized to use this
    app").setMimeType(ContentService.MimeType.TEXT)};
  Logger.log('user = '+user  )
  var ss =
    SpreadsheetApp.openById('0AnqSFd3iikE3dFBub2t1Ry1PaXJUMUVkSVVSemp
Cenc');
  var data = ss.getSheetByName('Farmer
    prices').getDataRange().getValues();
  var outString = '';
  for(var n=0 ; n<data.length ; ++n){
    if(data[n][0]==''){ continue };
    var dataRow = data[n][1]+','+data[n][4]+';\n';// \n is the
      "new line" character
    outString+=dataRow;// compose the output string
  }
    Logger.log('outString = '+outString);
    var result =
      ContentService.createTextOutput(outString).
setMimeType(ContentService.MimeType.CSV);//
      serve the string as a csv file to download
    return result;
}
```

In the preceding code, we get the parameter that has to be added to the URL using `url?user=username` and use it in the script to identify the user. If the parameter is wrong (or missing), we send an error message in readable text; otherwise, we send two columns of a spreadsheet in CSV format (that's again an interesting code snippet to keep in mind).

You can test this URL with parameter at `https://script.google.com/macros/s/AKfycbyPX58xpAbVH3Fa1iT10G2CY5eFGo0AHWYIbj8KH9PEShLUOaxC/exec?user=giovanni` and without a parameter at `https://script.google.com/macros/s/AKfycbyPX58xpAbVH3Fa1iT10G2CY5eFGo0AHWYIbj8KH9PEShLUOaxC/exec` and check the result as a downloaded `.csv` file.

You may feel that it's annoying to see the username in the URL and it is. So, let us use the Google URL Shortener service to make it less obvious (the URL with the parameter included):

`http://goo.gl/oUK8wr`

Not bad, is it? To be honest, there are a few shortcomings in using short URLs (read the Wikipedia article at `http://en.wikipedia.org/wiki/URL_shortening`); but in this specific use case, it is still very useful.

You can easily create one URL for every user and this will provide a very efficient data protection system.

Protecting your data (and your script)

We have seen in the previous section how to prevent an unauthorized user from accessing your web apps. However, in some cases, we would like to allow users to use the application, but not to be able to modify our script (even accidentally) or open a script-related document.

With reference to the first point, we should clarify again some aspects of file sharing and app sharing to be sure that there is no ambiguity in your understanding of the concepts:

- In standalone apps, the script doesn't need to be shared for a user to run the app (but, in spreadsheet- or document-embedded scripts, the permissions for the script are the same as those for the container).

- If an app is running on the **User accessing the web app** option, each file for which the script can read or write must be shared with that user too (or be public or shared with **Anyone with the link**).

- Note that the code itself doesn't need to be shared for an app to be shared. Don't share your code if it is not necessary.

- If the app is running with you as the user and owner of the script and files, the documents don't need to be shared.

Then the question is: how can we let an app access some data without sharing that source?

That will be the last example in this chapter and will use a special service called the `UrlFetch` service, documented at `https://developers.google.com/apps-script/reference/url-fetch/`.

The documentation states the following:

> *This service allows scripts to access other resources on the web by fetching URLs. A script can use the UrlFetch service to issue HTTP and HTTPS requests and receive responses. The UrlFetch service uses Google's network infrastructure for efficiency and scaling purposes.*

When we read the previously quoted description, we don't immediately think of using it to fetch spreadsheets, documents, or other Google services data, although it is the only truly reliable and safe way to use data without sharing the source.

The idea is to create a second app that runs as a service and deployed as running as me (so this app can access all your sources) and make it respond to external requests coming from the shared app that the user executes.

Let us imagine a typical situation: I write a script that creates a web app to collect information that I'd like to store in a spreadsheet. The app runs as the user executing it because it needs to get some information about them, so I would normally be forced to share the spreadsheet with them, but don't want them to go to that spreadsheet and see its content for privacy reasons.

We are going to write a short code to demonstrate the principle we'll use; the code shows the spreadsheet part that acts as a basic data server. The spreadsheet is not shared.

It expects a parameter with the row number, column number, mode (read or write), and a value if the mode is write.

It returns the value from the row/column cell of the spreadsheet when in read mode and writes a value in that cell if it's in the write mode.

 The following code is for demonstration only; it is completely inefficient as we have one request per value and will be very slow.

I chose that workflow for two reasons: it is simple and clear and you can easily look at the spreadsheet and actually see data being updated cell by cell in real time.

```
function doGet(e) {
  if(e.parameter.mode==null){return
    ContentService.createTextOutput("error, wrong
    request").setMimeType(ContentService.MimeType.TEXT)};
  var row = Number(e.parameter.row);
  var col = Number(e.parameter.col);
  var mode = e.parameter.mode;
```

```
    var value = e.parameter.value;
    var ss = SpreadsheetApp.openById('19FdtPgo3pAciO6-
gU6pZDyP7baiv4IBKvtW84xX639k');
    var sh = ss.getSheets()[0];
    if(mode=='read'){
      var sheetValue =  sh.getRange(row,col).getValue();
      Logger.log('value to send = '+sheetValue);
      var valToReturn =
        ContentService.createTextOutput(sheetValue).
setMimeType(ContentService.MimeType.TEXT);
      return valToReturn;
      }
    if(mode=='write'){
      sh.getRange(row, col).setValue(value);
      return ContentService.createTextOutput(value).
setMimeType(ContentService.MimeType.TEXT);
      }
    return ContentService.createTextOutput('error').
setMimeType(ContentService.MimeType.TEXT);
  }
  //for info: UrlFetchApp.fetch(url+'?row='+n+'&col='+m+'&mode=write&val
ue='+textBoxValue);
```

This code must be deployed as a web app that runs as you and that anyone can access, even an anonymous user. When you have the public URL, copy and paste it in the following second script.

 Don't use the development URL (.dev) because it is only available to the script editor(s) and the app sends an anonymous request so it won't work. Don't forget to authorize the script by running the doGet() function from the editor (this will request authorization and then fail because no parameters were present, but that is normal).

The following code shows the user UI part as a simple grid with two columns and a pair of buttons to read or write-to the spreadsheet; I added a small .gif image to show the script activity using a client handler to set it as visible, as previously explained:

```
var stylePanel = {'padding':'50px', 'background':'#FFA'};
var styleButton = {'padding':'5px', 'border-radius':'5px',
  'borderWidth':'1px', 'borderColor':'#DDD','fontSize':'12pt'};
var styleTextItalic =
  {'fontSize':'12pt','fontStyle':'italic','fontFamily':'arial,sans-
serif','color':'#F00'};
```

```
var styleTextNormal =
  {'fontSize':'12pt','fontStyle':'normal','fontFamily':'arial,sans-
serif','color':'#00F'};
var styleLabel = {'fontSize':'12pt','color':'#F00'};
var url =
  'https://script.google.com/macros/s/AKfycbxbtrK7BoUrGAz1wbkfEbZSE9_
HYWOabw4g79yK5-zhvwU0Y5c/exec';
;
function doGet() {
  var app = UiApp.createApplication().setTitle('url_fetch_demo');
  var panel = app.createVerticalPanel().
setStyleAttributes(stylePanel);
  var headers = ['Field Name','Your answer'];
  var grid = app.createGrid(7,2);
  var wait =
    app.createImage('https://dl.dropboxusercontent.com/u/211279/
loading3T.gif').setId('wait').setVisible(false);
  var handlerWrite =
    app.createServerHandler('writeSheet').addCallbackElement(grid);
  var handlerRead =
    app.createServerHandler('readSheet').addCallbackElement(grid);
  var Chandler =
    app.createClientHandler().forTargets(wait).setVisible(true);
  var buttonWrite = app.createButton('Write to
    Sheet',handlerWrite).addClickHandler(Chandler).setStyleAttributes
(styleButton);
  var buttonRead = app.createButton('Read from
    Sheet',handlerRead).addClickHandler(Chandler).setStyleAttributes(
styleButton);
  for(var n=1 ; n < 5 ; n++){
    for(var m=0 ; m < 2 ; m++){
      var textBox = app.createTextBox().setText('no
        value').setName('text'+n+'-'+m).setId('text'+n+'-'+m).setStyle
Attributes(styleTextNormal);
      if(m==0){textBox.setEnabled(false)};// left column is read only
      grid.setWidget(n,m,textBox);
    }
  }
  grid.setWidget(5,0,buttonRead).setWidget(5,1,buttonWrite).
setWidget(6,1,wait)
  .setWidget(0,0,app.createLabel(headers[0]).
setStyleAttributes(styleLabel))
  .setWidget(0,1,app.createLabel(headers[1]).setStyleAttributes(style
Label));
  app.add(panel.add(grid));
```

```
      return app;
  }


function writeSheet(e){
    var app = UiApp.getActiveApplication();
    app.getElementById('wait').setVisible(false);// hide the image when
we return
    for(var n=1 ; n < 5 ; n++){
      var textBoxValue = e.parameter['text'+n+'-1'];
      Logger.log(textBoxValue);
      var textBox = app.getElementById('text'+n+'-'+1).setStyleAttribute
s(styleTextItalic);//update only right column
      var write = UrlFetchApp.fetch(url+'?row='+n+'&col=2&mode=write&val
ue='+textBoxValue).getContentText();
      if(write!=textBoxValue){throw('comm error : response='+write)};
    }
    return app;
  }


function readSheet(e){
    var app = UiApp.getActiveApplication();
    app.getElementById('wait').setVisible(false);// hide the image when
we return

    for(var n=1 ; n < 5 ; n++){
      for(var m=0 ; m < 2 ; m++){
        var textBox = app.getElementById('text'+n+'-'+m).setStyleAttribu
tes(styleTextNormal);
        var textValue = UrlFetchApp.fetch(url+'?row='+n+'&col='+(m+1)+'&
mode=read').getContentText()
        Logger.log(textValue);
        textBox.setText(textValue);
      }
    }
    return app;
  }
```

An Online demo app can be found at the following URL:

https://script.google.com/macros/s/AKfycbyApSkRkea7oZ7CWGUfvBCZLFjVqH
JBdxwmDKd-OiWbSzYOYntG/exec

The following screenshot shows the user interface:

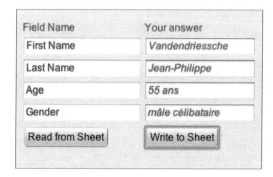

The following screenshot shows the private spreadsheet:

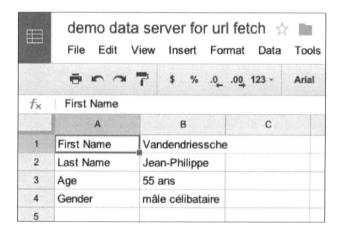

A Demo spreadsheet in the view-only mode can be found at `https://docs.google.com/spreadsheets/d/19FdtPgo3pAciO6-gU6pZDyP7baiv4IBKvtW84xX639k/edit?usp=sharing`.

If you intend to use such a dual-app configuration in real life, I'd suggest that you write the code differently as you probably won't spend your time looking at the spreadsheet! The idea is to reduce the number of calls from one app to another so that it would update much faster.

In the data server script, get the whole data range and run it using a JSON array of string values within that range and in the user interface, send a request/submit for the whole data array and update all the cells in one `setValues()` function.

The next script is the second version of this same script using batch read and write and a single `urlFetch` service to exchange all the data; it is definitely faster.

The code is not so different, except that I had to use special encoding to pass the JSON as a parameter because it contains invalid characters. I used base64 encoding/decoding, but there are probably other (or better) approaches.

You can try both versions with the test URLs and see the speed difference.

Please note that even though I have initially embedded this code in a spreadsheet (for my own comfort in that I won't have to look for the data spreadsheet), you could also use an independent script file instead. It is a typical example of a standalone web app without any user interface, meaning that it runs as a service on its own.

The data server code is as follows:

```
function doGet(e) {
  if(e.parameter.mode==null){return
    ContentService.createTextOutput("error, wrong
    request").setMimeType(ContentService.MimeType.TEXT)};
  var mode = e.parameter.mode;
  var value = e.parameter.value;
  var ss =
    SpreadsheetApp.openById('1yad5sZZt-X6bIftpR--
OSyf3VZWf3Jxx8UJBhh7Arwg');
  var sh = ss.getSheets()[0];
  if(mode=='read'){
      var sheetValues =   sh.getDataRange().getValues();// get data
from sheet
      var valToReturn =
        ContentService.createTextOutput(JSON.stringify(sheetValues)).
setMimeType(ContentService.MimeType.JSON);
      return valToReturn;// send it as JSON string
      }
  if(mode=='write'){
      var val =
        Utilities.base64Decode(value,Utilities.Charset.UTF_8);//
decode base64 and get an array of numbers
      Logger.log(val);// see it !
      var stringVal = ''; // create an empty string
      for(var n in val){
          stringVal += String.fromCharCode(val[n]);// add each
character in turn
      }
      var sheetValues =
        JSON.parse(stringVal);// convert the string into an object (2D
array)
      Logger.log(sheetValues);// check result
```

```
    sh.getRange(1,1,sheetValues.length,sheetValues[0].length).
setValues(sheetValues);// update the sheet
      return ContentService.createTextOutput(JSON.
stringify(sheetValues)).setMimeType(ContentService.MimeType.JSON);//
send back the result as a string
    }
  return ContentService.createTextOutput('error').
setMimeType(ContentService.MimeType.TEXT);// in case mode is not
'read' nor 'write'... should not happen !
}
```

The following user UI code has almost the same doGet() function, except that I
added a numRow parameter to choose the number of rows in the grid, so you can
create long grids. You will note that the execution time won't increase with an
increase in the cell count. The comments are in the code.

```
var stylePanel = {'padding':'50px', 'background':'#FFA'};
var styleButton = {'padding':'5px', 'border-radius':'5px',
  'borderWidth':'1px', 'borderColor':'#DDD','fontSize':'12pt'};
var styleTextItalic =
  {'fontSize':'12pt','fontStyle':'italic','fontFamily':'arial,sans-
serif','color':'#F00'};
var styleTextNormal =
  {'fontSize':'12pt','fontStyle':'normal','fontFamily':'arial,sans-
serif','color':'#00F'};
var styleLabel = {'fontSize':'12pt','color':'#F00'};
var url =
  'https://script.google.com/macros/s/AKfycbwPioVjYMSrmhKnJOaF2GG83dns
tLWI7isU9SF1vxPV8td-g9E7/exec';
var numRow = 21;// the number of rows in the grid = number of rows in
the SS + 1
;
function doGet() {
  var app = UiApp.createApplication().setTitle('url_fetch_demo');
  var panel =
    app.createVerticalPanel().setStyleAttributes(stylePanel);
  var headers = ['Field Name','Your answer'];// grid title
  var grid = app.createGrid(numRow+2,2);// create the grid with right
size
  var wait =
    app.createImage('https://dl.dropboxusercontent.com/u/211279/
loading3T.gif').setId('wait').setVisible(false);// get a spinner image
in animated gif
  var handlerWrite =
    app.createServerHandler('writeSheet').addCallbackElement(grid);//
2 handlers for the buttons
```

```
  var handlerRead =
    app.createServerHandler('readSheet').addCallbackElement(grid);
  var Chandler =
    app.createClientHandler().forTargets(wait).setVisible(true);// a
client handler for the spinner
  var buttonWrite = app.createButton('Write to
    Sheet',handlerWrite).addClickHandler(Chandler).setStyleAttributes
(styleButton);
  var buttonRead = app.createButton('Read from
    Sheet',handlerRead).addClickHandler(Chandler).setStyleAttributes(
styleButton);
  for(var n=1 ; n < numRow ; n++){
      for(var m=0 ; m < 2 ; m++){ // create all the textBoxes with
names & IDs
          var textBox = app.createTextBox().setText('no
            value').setName('text'+n+'-'+m).setId('text'+n+'-'+m).setS
tyleAttributes(styleTextNormal);
      //if(m==0){textBox.setEnabled(false)};// prevent writing to left
column (optional)
          grid.setWidget(n,m,textBox);// place widgets
      }
  }
  grid.setWidget(numRow,0,buttonRead).setWidget(numRow,1,buttonWrite).
setWidget(numRow+1,1,wait) // place buttons
  .setWidget(0,0,app.createLabel(headers[0]).
setStyleAttributes(styleLabel)) // and headers
  .setWidget(0,1,app.createLabel(headers[1]).setStyleAttributes(style
Label));
  app.add(panel.add(grid));
  return app; // show Ui
}


function writeSheet(e){
  var app = UiApp.getActiveApplication();
  app.getElementById('wait').setVisible(false);// spinner will be
hidden when fct returns
  var dataArrayImage = [];// an array to get typed values
  for(var n=1 ; n < numRow ; n++){
      var row=[];
    for(var m=0 ; m < 2 ; m++){
          row.push(e.parameter['text'+n+'-'+m]); // get every value in
every "cell"
          var textBox = app.getElementById('text'+n+'-'+m).setStyleAtt
ributes(styleTextItalic);// update "cells" style
```

```
        //textBox.setText('written value = '+e.parameter['text'+n+'-
'+m]);// rewrite to the cells - not usefull but serves to check while
debugging
        }
     dataArrayImage.push(row);// store one row(=2cells)
  }
  var UiValues = JSON.stringify(dataArrayImage);// stringfy the array
  var newValues = url+'?mode=write&value='+Utilities.
base64Encode(UiValues,Utilities.Charset.UTF_8);// add to URL &
parameters+ encode in pure ASCII characters
  Logger.log(newValues);// check in logger
  var check = UrlFetchApp.fetch(newValues).getContent();// get back
the result
  Logger.log(check);// check result = newValues sent back in bytes
format
  return app;//update Ui
}


function readSheet(e){
  var app = UiApp.getActiveApplication();
  app.getElementById('wait').setVisible(false);
  var returnedValue = UrlFetchApp.fetch(url+'?mode=read').
getContentText();// get data from server
  Logger.log(returnedValue);// check values
  var sheetValues = JSON.parse(returnedValue);
  for(var n=1 ; n < numRow ; n++){
     for(var m=0 ; m < 2 ; m++){
        var textBox = app.getElementById('text'+n+'-'+m).setStyleAtt
ributes(styleTextNormal);
        textBox.setText(sheetValues[n-1][m]);// iterate and update
cells values
     }
  }
return app;// update Ui
  }
```

The test URL is as follows:

```
https://script.google.com/macros/s/
AKfycbzYzwX9lTGTvy0gVdUJlChLP5626d_loAnZNvaoisaxupGPAd4/exec
```

Summary

If we consider Google Apps Script as a toolbox with plenty of different tools, the tools we introduced in this chapter are probably the most powerful and useful.

There will indeed be many occasions when we may want to execute some simple (or not) tasks without using a full-featured spreadsheet: standalone web apps are the solution. Since they can easily be shared across offices or with other users, they also present us with a good way to preserve our privacy.

It might seem a bit complicated, but after a short while, we get pretty familiar with their structure and simple apps take only a few minutes to write.

Now that we understand this new possibility, why not try to integrate UIs in other documents? That will be the focus of the next chapter.

7

Using User Interfaces in Spreadsheets and Documents

There are many situations where we need to present some data from within a spreadsheet or a document but where the standard user interface is not really appropriate. For example, you have a logging sheet of all the visitors of an exhibition and you'd like to show an average count of the people that were present at this exhibition on a given day. It is of course possible to calculate this in a spreadsheet and decide which cell shows this value, but suppose you want to be able to get some variant of this and get a mean value for the exhibition duration; what are you going to do? Create a new cell with another result, and again come up against the need to add a description cell somewhere for identification purposes.

Let's check out an easier solution for this using what we just learned in the previous chapter.

Pop ups

Pop ups are a simple user interface that you could call from a menu or a drawing / image, that presents your result in the form of a couple of listboxes from which you can select the result you want.

Here is a screenshot of such a UI that I created to calculate the working hours of our teachers across three grades and different courses, with horizontal and vertical totals.

The preceding UI panel comes up as a pop-up window and reads data from the current spreadsheet. I don't need to change the data in any way, nor change the layout of my sheet; everything is done from the UI, and I can call it whenever I need it. This is really comfortable to use, but it uses a lot of external resources, such as teacher calendars and custom resources, so it does not become a valid candidate as a demo script.

Let us take a simpler example to show how we can create and use this UI.

The spreadsheet we use here is the main interface of a complete online reservation tool for any public show. After we have filled a couple of cells with titles and descriptions, it will create a form that we can publish on the Web. All the form answers will get inserted into a logger sheet that typically looks as illustrated in the following screenshot:

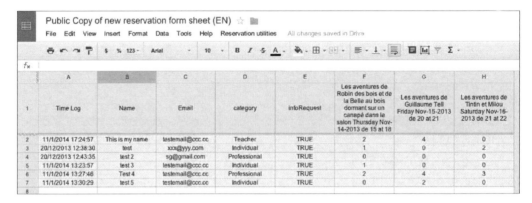

In this example, I have only six responses so it's rather easy to read; but when I get hundreds of them, it won't be easy anymore.

The UI looks like the following screenshot:

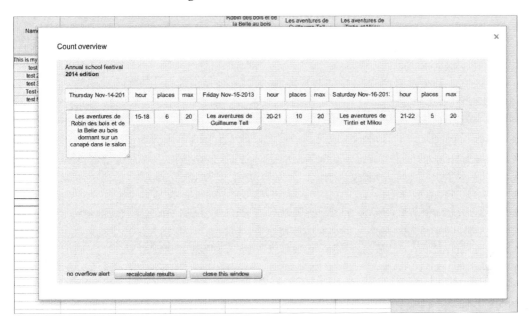

In this UI, we can view everything we need in one glance; even if we were to have more events and many more responses, it would automatically resize its columns to fit the best possible way.

Now let's have a look at the code:

```
function countData(){
    var day = ScriptProperties.getProperty('day').split('|');
    var numQ = ScriptProperties.getProperty('numQuestion');
    var genTitle = ScriptProperties.getProperty('genTitle');
    var stHour = ScriptProperties.getProperty('stHour').split('|');
    var endHour = ScriptProperties.getProperty('endHour').split('|');
    var title = ScriptProperties.getProperty('title').split('|');
    var descr = ScriptProperties.getProperty('descr').split('|');
    var resNum = ScriptProperties.getProperty('resNum').split('|');
    var resMax = ScriptProperties.getProperty('resMax').split('|');
```

The parameters of the current form are stored in `ScriptProperties`, a convenient place for a small amount of information.

```
var data = logSheet.getDataRange().getValues();//data come from the
logSheet
var resVal = [];
for(var d=0;d<day.length;++d){
  var resCount = 0;
  for(var n=1;n<data.length;++n){resCount+=Number(data[n][(d+5)])};
  resVal.push(resCount);
}
ScriptProperties.setProperty('resVal',resVal.join('|'));
var uniqueDay = [];
var ud = 0;
uniqueDay.push(day[0]);
for(var d=1;d<day.length;++d){
  if(day[d]!=uniqueDay[ud]){uniqueDay.push(day[d]);ud++}
}
Logger.log(uniqueDay+' length='+uniqueDay.length);
```

In this first part, we examine how many events we have for each day and how many responses we received so that we can build our UI with the right column size. We decided not to exceed a width of 900 pixels so that it remains visible even on smaller screens (tablets, for example). The following code depicts this:

```
var frameWidth = 300*uniqueDay.length.toString();
if(frameWidth>900){frameWidth=900};
var app = UiApp.createApplication().setTitle('Count overview').
setHeight(480).setWidth(frameWidth+50).setStyleAttribute('background'
,'#ffffaa');
var panel = app.createVerticalPanel().setStyleAttributes(styleCalc);
var panelV = app.createVerticalPanel().
setStyleAttributes(styleCalc);
var panelH = app.createHorizontalPanel().
setStyleAttributes(styleCalc).setStyleAttribute('margin-left','7px');
var scroll = app.createScrollPanel().setWidth(frameWidth+25).
setHeight('400');
panel.add(panelV).add(panelH);
scroll.add(panel);
var colIdx = [];
var colPanel = [];
var alertCount = 0;
var titleRow = app.createHorizontalPanel();
```

```
  app.add(app.createHTML(genTitle).setStyleAttributes({'padding':'8px'
,'margin-left':'10px'}));
  panelV.add(titleRow.setStyleAttribute('padding-left','6px'));
  for(var c=0;c<uniqueDay.length;c++){titleRow.add(app.
createTextBox().setText(uniqueDay[c])
  .setStyleAttributes(styleRow).setReadOnly(true).setWidth('140'))
  .add(app.createTextBox().setText('hour')
  .setStyleAttributes(styleRow)
  .setReadOnly(true).setWidth('55'))
 .add(app.createTextBox().setText('places')
  .setStyleAttributes(styleRow).setReadOnly(true)
  .setWidth('55')).add(app.createTextBox().setText('max')
  .setStyleAttributes(styleRow).setReadOnly(true).setWidth('40')) ;
    }
```

The styles were defined outside the function in the preceding code so as to keep the code tidy.

```
  for(var u=0;u<uniqueDay.length;u++){colIdx.push(0) ; colPanel.
push(app.createVerticalPanel()) ; panelH.add(colPanel[u])};
  for(var u=0;u<uniqueDay.length;u++){
    for(var d=0;d<day.length;++d){if(day[d]==uniqueDay[u])
{colIdx[d]=u}}
  }
  for(var d=0;d<day.length;++d){
    Logger.log(' d='+d+'  title[d]:'+title[d]+' in column '+colIdx[d])
  }
  for(var d=0;d<day.length;++d){
    var alert = '#ffffde';
    if(resVal[d]>=resMax[d]){alert='orange' ; alertCount++}
    var row = app.createHorizontalPanel().add(app.createTextArea()
  .setText(title[d]).setStyleAttributes(styleRow)
  .setReadOnly(true).setWidth('140')).add(app.createTextBox()
  .setText(stHour[d]+'-'+endHour[d])
  .setStyleAttributes(styleRow).setReadOnly(true).setWidth('55'))
   .add(app.createTextBox().setText(resVal[d])
  .setStyleAttributes(styleRow)
  .setStyleAttribute('background',alert)
  .setReadOnly(true).setWidth('55').setId('resVal'+d))
  .add(app.createTextBox().setText(resMax[d])
  .setStyleAttributes(styleRow).setReadOnly(true).setWidth('40')) ;
    colPanel[colIdx[d]].add(row);
//  Logger.log('colPanel['+colIdx[d]+'].add(row)')
  }
```

In the preceding code, we count the places on the fly and check if it does not exceed the limits. If it did, we display an alert message and set an orange background for the faulty items.

```
var commentMsg = "no overflow alert";
if(alertCount>0){commentMsg = alertCount+" overflow alert(s)   !
(orange cell(s)"};
var comment = app.createHTML(commentMsg).setId('comment');
if(alertCount>0){comment.setStyleAttributes(stylHeader)}
else{comment.setStyleAttributes(styleDate)};
var rHandler = app.createServerHandler('refresh').
addCallbackElement(panel);
var refresh = app.createButton('recalculate results', rHandler).
setStyleAttributes({'padding':'2px','border-radius':'4px'}).
setWidth('160');
var rcHandler = app.createServerHandler('closeApp');
var closAp = app.createButton('close this window', rcHandler)
.setStyleAttributes({'padding':'2px','border-radius':'4px'}).
setWidth('160');
```

A pair of buttons allows us to refresh (to redo the counting) and close the UI respectively. This is done using the preceding code snippet.

```
app.add(scroll).add(app.createHorizontalPanel()
.add(comment).add(refresh).add(closAp)
.setStyleAttributes({'margin-left':'14px'}));
SpreadsheetApp.getActiveSpreadsheet().show(app);// show app
var bgUser = logSheet.getRange(1,1,logSheet.getLastRow(),logSheet.
getLastColumn()).getBackgrounds();
var colorUser = logSheet.getRange(1,1,logSheet.
getLastRow(),logSheet.getLastColumn()).getFontColors();
for(var n=1 ; n<bgUser.length;++n){
  for(var c in bgUser[n]){
    if(c!=2){
      bgUser[n][c]='#eeffee'
      colorUser[n][c]='#000000'
    }
  }
}
logSheet.getRange(1,1,logSheet.getLastRow(),logSheet.
getLastColumn()).setBackgrounds(bgUser);
logSheet.getRange(1,1,logSheet.getLastRow(),logSheet.
getLastColumn()).setFontColors(colorUser);
}
```

We change the background in the logger sheet as well so that we know that the colored rows were part of the count at that moment (other responses might have come in while we were checking), as shown in the preceding code.

```
function closeApp(){
  var app = UIApp.getActiveApplication();
  return(app.close())
}
```

The small function in the preceding code is used to close the UI and go back to the normal spreadsheet view.

As you can see, there is nothing too difficult to follow in the code snippets explained earlier; there are only about 80 lines of code in the script editor that result in a very convenient interface.

The entire code and template spreadsheet are available in view mode at the following link:

```
https://docs.google.com/spreadsheet/ccc?key=0AnqSFd3iikE3dFluVktBVFJr
Mkd5WUtxYWU2ZlQtUFE&usp=sharing
```

There are many other functions in this script: to generate the form's UI, to send confirmation e-mails, and to generate daily lists in alphabetical order for easy "real-life checks" using a paper and a pencil. None of these functions are really complicated, but the whole script is pretty long (it has 540 lines of code) and wouldn't fit in here for practical reasons.

 The script file has comments that explain every method we have used, so anyone should be able to understand it easily.

One detail I'd like to mention is about the appearance of this form. I mentioned in *Chapter 2, Create and Manipulate Forms,* that you could design your own forms using a UI service or HTML service (this is a good example) to avoid having the Google logo and name on your form.

Indeed, there is no Google logo on the form we generated; however, users will see a warning message as shown in the following screenshot:

This application was created by another user, not by Google.

This, I admit, is also annoying (although the user can dismiss it), but we can't do anything about it. Google considers it has to exclude its responsibility in case a script functions incorrectly.

Also, the URL of the form is a bit long but, as we learned before, we can use a URL Shortener service to make it shorter: `http://goo.gl/jrtjlJ`. All in all, this solution to use a web app to create forms is, in my humble opinion, quite satisfying.

This example shows all the possible ways to utilize user interfaces in spreadsheets, such as custom menus, browser pop ups, and custom UIs, but text documents, because they appear later in history, have even more ways to implement custom user interfaces.

Sidebars

Sidebars are only available in Google text documents and in form creation UIs. This feature has been introduced quite recently and offers a wide array of possible applications.

We used a very basic example of this in *Chapter 2, Create and Manipulate Forms*, to show a sample of the last form responses, but we can make it a lot more useful and attractive if we wish.

An impressive example was published a few months ago by a Google engineer on GitHub (`https://github.com/google/google-apps-script-samples/tree/master/cursor_inspector`).

Cursor Inspector is a script that shows the content and properties of the selected text in a sidebar in a document. From there on, we can imagine all sorts of developments: automatic data insertion in text, contextual help, and so on.

The code of this demo uses Google Apps Script and jQuery in a JavaScript client and is far from simple, but results in something awesome. I can't recommend enough that you give it a try.

The small test we are going to try here is simpler in many aspects and is also shorter, but it uses a few funny and interesting tricks.

Everybody knows that Google Docs has an integrated chat feature that allows editors to chat in real time while they are both active on the same document. A few months ago, someone on the Stack Overflow forum asked for an equivalent feature because he apparently couldn't use it due to some browser limitations (http://stackoverflow.com/questions/19648798/creating-a-basic-chatbar/19653610#19653610). I found the request rather funny, so I participated in the thread, and we finally came to a working solution that I will show here with a couple of improvements as an example of a "live" UI in a text document's sidebar.

```
function onOpen() {
  DocumentApp.getUI().createMenu('Chat Utilities')
  .addItem('Open Chat', 'createChatBox')
  .addItem('Show your current ID','showUser')
  .addItem('Change your user name', 'setUserName')
  .addToUI();
}
```

A simple onOpen function is used to create a menu in the document as shown in the preceding code.

```
function createChatBox(){
  ScriptProperties.setProperty('chatContent','');
  var app = UIApp.createApplication().setWidth(252);
  app.setTitle("Chat Bar");
  var vPanel = app.createVerticalPanel().setId('chatPanel').
setWidth('100%');
  var chatHandler = app.createServerHandler("sayChat").
addCallbackElement(vPanel);
  var textArea = app.createTextArea().setId('chatBox').
setName('chatBox').setReadOnly(true).setText('').setSize('250px',
'450px');
  var textBox = app.createTextArea().setId('messageBox').
setName('messageBox').setText('Start chat...').setPixelSize(250,100).
setStyleAttributes({'padding':'5px','background':'#ffffcc'}).addKeyPre
ssHandler(chatHandler);
  var clearTextBoxClientHandler = app.createClientHandler().
forTargets(textBox).setText('');
  textBox.addClickHandler(clearTextBoxClientHandler);// a
ClientHandler to delete old text when we click the textArea
  var chatButton = app.createButton().setId("sayButton").
setText("Say!").addMouseUpHandler(chatHandler);
```

The preceding part of the code is a classical UiApp code with a button and two text areas, one to see the conversation (as read only) and a second to actually type in the messages. The issue at this point was to find a way to update the conversation panel in every instance of the script in different documents at the same moment so that each user would see the new messages without having to do anything.

As I already mentioned before, each instance of a script is new and completely ignores what is happening in another instance, so we had to use a common memory where we could store the messages. Doing this was simple as `ScriptProperties` belongs to the script (that is the document), so each document user has access to it; it is typically a shared resource.

On the other hand, each UI is unique for each user, and the only way to actually update the UI is to use a handler function.

However, as we have seen before, a handler function needs a trigger, generally some action from the user: a mouse click or the pressing of a key.

In this case, we don't want the user to do anything; he should receive the chat messages automatically.

What I used here is a special property of the checkbox widget (see the documentation at `https://developers.google.com/apps-script/reference/ui/check-box?hl=fr-FR#setValue(Boolean,Boolean)` that is able to fire an event when its value is changed programmatically.

Using this feature, we can easily create a timer based on a positive feedback loop on this checkbox. After a chosen delay, the handler function changes the checkbox value that in turn triggers the handler function, and so on.

We intentionally limit the number of cycles to let it work for a "reasonable" amount of time and stop after a certain period of inactivity. (In this test version, the limit is set to 30 seconds so that we see it working without having to wait for 5 minutes.) The following code depicts this:

```
    var chkHandler = app.createServerHandler('autoUpdate').
addCallbackElement(vPanel);
    var chk = app.createCheckBox().setId('chk').addValueChangeHandler(c
hkHandler);
    vPanel.add(textArea);
    vPanel.add(textBox);
    vPanel.add(chatButton);
    vPanel.add(chk);
    app.add(vPanel);
```

```
  DocumentApp.getUI().showSidebar(app);
  return app;
}


function sayChat(e){
  var app = UiApp.getActiveApplication();
  var user = '['+getCurrentUser()+'] : ';
  if(e.parameter.messageBox=="You have been put offline because you
didn't type anything for more than 5 minutes..., please click here to
refresh the conversation"){
    app.getElementById("chatBox").setText(content);// refresh chatBox
    app.getElementById('messageBox').setText('');// clear messageBox
    ScriptProperties.setProperty('chatTimer',0);// reset counter
    return app;
  }
  if(e.parameter.source=='messageBox'&&e.parameter.keyCode!=13){return
app};// if we are simply typing a message then return immediately
  var content = ScriptProperties.getProperty('chatContent');
  ScriptProperties.setProperty('chatContent',content+"\n"+user+e.
parameter.messageBox);// store the conversation with user names
  app.getElementById("chatBox").setText(content+"\n"+user+e.parameter.
messageBox+'\n');// update the conversation area
  app.getElementById('messageBox').setText('');// and clear the
message area
  app.getElementById('chk').setValue(true,true);// start the timer
  ScriptProperties.setProperty('chatTimer',0);// initialize the
counter
  return app;
}
```

We use `e.parameter.source` to identify which event caused the handler to be triggered because the same handler applies to the "say" button and the message's text area. The `source` parameter in e tells us if it is a button or a text area.

```
function autoUpdate(){ // this function called on checkBox event
  var app = UiApp.getActiveApplication();
  var content = ScriptProperties.getProperty('chatContent');
  var counter = Number(ScriptProperties.getProperty('chatTimer'));
  ++counter;// increment counter
  if(counter>30){ // if > limit then stop the timer, change this value
to get a longer delay
    app.getElementById('chk').setValue(false);
    app.getElementById('messageBox').setText("You have been put
offline because you didn't type anything for more than 5 minutes...,
please click here to refresh the conversation");
```

```
      return app;
    } ; // else update the chat Area
    ScriptProperties.setProperty('chatTimer',counter);// store the
counter value
    var content = ScriptProperties.getProperty('chatContent');
    app.getElementById("chatBox").setText(content+'*'); // the * is
there only for test purpose
    app.getElementById('chk').setValue(false);
    Utilities.sleep(950);// wait 950 millisec to get approximately a one
second total delay
    app.getElementById('chk').setValue(true,true).setText('timer =
'+counter);// create a new event (= activate the positive feedBack
loop)
    return app;// update the UI
}


function showUser(){
    DocumentApp.getUi().alert("Your userId is: "+getCurrentUser());
}


function getCurrentUser(){
    var email = Session.getEffectiveUser().getEmail();
    var user = UserProperties.getProperty('user')==null ||
UserProperties.getProperty('user')=='' ? email.substring(0,email.
indexOf("@")) : UserProperties.getProperty('user');
    return user;
}
```

In the following code, the setUserName() function allows us to change the
username. The shown username is stored in UserProperties, which is different
for every user, of course. When we change this name, it shows a message in the
chat messages area to warn every other user about this (no way to cheat!).

```
function setUserName(){
    var oldName = getCurrentUser();
    var user = DocumentApp.getUi().prompt('Please enter your desired
user name as it will be shown\n(old name was '+oldName+', default is
your mail ID)', DocumentApp.getUi().ButtonSet.OK_CANCEL);
    if(user.getSelectedButton() == DocumentApp.getUi().Button.CANCEL)
return;
    ScriptProperties.setProperty('chatContent','\n['+oldName+'] is
changing his user name to ['+user.getResponseText()+']\n');// show the
new name along with a warning in the chat history
    UserProperties.setProperty('user',user.getResponseText());// store
the new user name
}
```

If no name has been defined, the username will default to the user's e-mail ID and be stored for later use.

Note that this last function uses a simplified if/then syntax without braces. JavaScript accepts this simplified form but it makes the code less easy to read, so I'd recommend that you keep using normal syntax with parentheses and braces.

The document with the embedded script is viewable as a shared document at the following link:

```
https://docs.google.com/document/d/1ZEHXFXn5zH8AfnMrImtrQmFoRD1m1PNuq
7lnUC8YABI/edit?usp=sharing
```

Summary

We can see that there are many use cases where a simple UI can at least simplify our work with spreadsheets and documents, either by showing data in a way that is not directly available or by adding extra functionalities.

We can also use the UiApp service or HTML service to create UIs; the latter allows us to create more fancy user interfaces if we are using third-party libraries.

Of course, this means that we'll need to learn a lot of new techniques. The complete documentation about jQuery is about 300 pages long (`http://forum.jquery.com/topic/jquery-1-7-reference-documentation-as-a-pdf`), and I'm not even sure that reading it entirely would be sufficient to use it easily. However, as we shall see in the next chapter, the learning process can be gradual.

8

How to Expand your Knowledge

One of the most frequently asked questions on help forums probably is, "How can I learn Google Apps Script?" The answer is almost always the same: learn JavaScript and follow the numerous tutorials available on the Internet.

No doubt, it is one of the possible ways to learn but it is also one of the most difficult ways. I shall express my opinion on that subject at the end of this chapter, but let us first summarize what we really need to be able to use Google Apps Script efficiently.

The first and most important thing we must have is a clear idea of what we want to achieve.

This seems a bit silly because we think, "Oh well, of course I know what I want; I just don't know how to do it!"

As a matter of fact, this is often not the case. Let us have an example: a colleague asked me recently how he could count the time he was spending at school for meetings and other administrative tasks, not taking into account his hours as a teacher.

This was supposed to be a simple problem as everyone in our school has a personal calendar in which all the events that we are invited to are recorded.

So, he began to search for a way to collect every possible event from his calendar to a spreadsheet and from there—since he can definitely use a spreadsheet—he intended to do some data filtering to get the result he wanted.

I told him to have a look at the Google Apps Script documentation and see what tools he had, to pick up data from calendars and import them into a spreadsheet.

A few days later, he came back to me complaining that he didn't find any appropriate methods to do what he needs to.

And, in a way, he was right; nowhere is such a workflow explained and it is actually not surprising. One can't imagine compiling all the possible workflows into a single help resource; there are definitely too many different use cases, each of them needing a particular approach. We had a discussion where I told him to think about his research as a series of simple and accurate parts and steps before trying to get the whole process in one stroke.

The following is what he told me another few days later:

"I knew nothing about this macro language, so I discovered that it is based on JavaScript with the addition of Google's own services that use a similar syntax and that the whole thing is composed of functions calling each other and having parameters. Then, I examined the calendar service and saw that it needs so-called date objects to choose a start and end date. Date object methods are pretty well explained on Mozilla's page, so once I got that I had an array of events, I thought what the heck is an array of objects? You gave me the link to this w3schools site, so I took a look at their definition; that was enough for me to go further and discover that I could use a loop to handle each event separately. Google documentation shows all the methods to get events details; that part was easy and now I have all my calendar events with dates, hours, description, title.
All of it! I tell you."

I'm not going to transcribe all of our conversation—it finally took a couple of hours—but towards the end, he was describing the process so well that the actual writing of his script was almost just a formality.

With the help of the **Content assist** (autocomplete) feature of the script editor and a couple of browser tabs left open on JavaScript and Google documentation, he managed to write his script in one day.

Of course, the script was not perfect and by no way optimized his speed or gave nice-looking results, but it worked and he had the data he was looking for.

At that point, he could post his script on a help forum if something went wrong or try to improve another version if he's a perfectionist, but that depends only on his will to go further or not.

This experience is not far from what I mentioned in the Preface about my own journey in the world of Google Apps Script; the only difference is that I took so much pleasure in it that I decided to continue to learn and explore all the fields of application, not because I'm smarter than anyone but because when I discover something, it always brings me to something else that I didn't know and could be so useful!

As a conclusion for this part, I would simply say one thing: you will learn what you need.

If you don't need it, don't try to learn it as you will forget it faster than you learned it.

If you do, then be prepared to need something else right after; it is an endless journey!

JavaScript versus Google Apps Script

The following is stated on the overview of Google Apps Script documentation page:

> *Google Apps Script is a scripting language based on JavaScript that lets you do new and cool things with Google Apps like Docs, Sheets, and Forms.*

They should use a bigger typeface to make it more visible!

The keyword here is *based on JavaScript* because it does indeed use most of the JavaScript Version 1.6 (with some portions of Version 1.7 and Version 1.8) and its general syntax. But, it has so many other methods that knowing only JavaScript is clearly not sufficient to use it adequately.

I would even say that you can learn it step-by-step when you need it, looking for information on a specific item each time you use a new type of object.

In *Chapter 1, Enhancing Spreadsheets*, we looked at the very first function presented in this book using that method (if you remember). The following is the code that was used:

```
function myAgeInHours(){
  var myBirthDate = new Date('1958/02/19 02:00:00').getTime();
  myBirthDate = parseInt(myBirthDate/3600000, 10);
  var today = parseInt(new Date().getTime()/3600000, 10);
  return today-myBirthDate;
}
```

We looked at the documentation about the Date object to find the getTime() method and then found parseInt to get the integer part of the result.

Well, I'm convinced that this approach is more efficient than spending hours on a site or in a book that shows all JavaScript information from A to Z. We have the opportunity to have powerful search engines in our browsers, so let's use them; they always find the answer for us in less time than it takes to write the question.

Concerning methods specific to Google Apps Script, I think the approach should be different.

The Google API documentation is pretty well organized and is full of code examples that clearly show us how to use almost every single method.

If we start a project in a spreadsheet, it is a good idea to carefully read the section about spreadsheets (`https://developers.google.com/apps-script/reference/spreadsheet`) at least once and just check if what it says makes any sense.

For example, in the `Sheet` class, I found this description: **Returns the range with the top left cell at the given coordinates, and with the given number of rows.**

The following screenshot displays the same description:

getRange(row, column, numRows)	Range	Returns the range with the top left cell at the given coordinates, and with the given number of rows.

If I understand what range and co-ordinates are, then I probably know enough to be able to use that method (`getRange(row, column, numRows`) or a similar one.

You want me to tell you the truth? I didn't know we could get a range this way by simply defining the top-left cell and just the number of rows (only three parameters.). I always use the next one in the list, which is shown as follows:

getRange(row, column, numRows, numColumns)	Range	Returns the range with the top left cell at the given coordinates with the given number of rows and columns.

The description says: **Returns the range with the top left cell at the given coordinates with the given number of rows and columns**.

So after all this time I spent on dozens of spreadsheet scripts, there still are methods that I can't even imagine exist!

That's actually a nice confirmation of what I was suggesting: one doesn't need to know everything to be able to use it but it's always a good idea to read the docs from time to time.

Infinite resources

As I have already mentioned a few times, JavaScript is a very popular language; there are thousands of websites that show us examples and explain methods and functions.

We must add all the forums and Q&A sites that return many results when we search something on Google to these websites (or any other search engine), and that is actually an unforeseen difficulty.

It happens quite often that we find false information or code snippets that simply don't work, either because they have typos in them or they are so badly written that they work only in a very specific and peculiar situation.

My personal solution is to use only a couple of websites and perform a search on their search engine, avoiding all the sources I'm not sure of. Maybe I miss something at times, but at least the information I get is trustworthy.

Last but certainly not least, the help forum recommended by the Google Apps Script team, `http://stackoverflow.com/questions/tagged/google-apps-script` (with the **google-apps-script** tag), is certainly the best resource that is available.

With more than 5000 questions (as of January, 2014), the help forum probably has threads about every possible use case and an important part of it has answers as well.

There are of course other interesting tags: JavaScript, Google docs, Google spreadsheets, and a few even more specific ones.

I have rarely seen really bad answers—although it does happen sometimes—simply because so many people read these posts that they generally flag or comment answers that show wrong information. There are also people from Google that regularly keep an eye on it and clarify any ambiguous response.

Being a newbie is, by definition, temporary

When I began to use Google spreadsheets and scripts, I found the Google Group Help forum (which does not exist anymore) an invaluable source of information and help, so I asked dozens of questions—some of them very basic and naive—and always got answers.

After a while, since I was spending hours on this forum reading about every post I found, I began to answer too. I was so proud of being able to answer a question!

It was almost like passing an examination; I knew that one of the experts there was going to read what I wrote and evaluate my knowledge; quite stressful but also satisfying when you don't fail!

So after a couple of months I gained my first level point (on the Google Group forum, there are no reputation points but levels, starting from 1 for new arriving members up to **TC** (**Top Contributors**), whose level is unknown but is generally more than 15 or 20; anyway, that's not important).

That little story is just a way to encourage any beginner to spend some time on this forum and consider every question as a challenge and try to answer it.

Of course, there is no need to publish your answer every time as there are chances that you may get it all wrong, but just use this as an exercise that will give you more and more expertise.

From time to time, you'll be able to be the first or best answerer and gain a few reputation points; consider it as a game, just a funny game where all you can finally win is knowledge and all you can lose is your newbie status—not a bad deal after all!

Try to find your own best learning method

I'm certainly not pretending that I know the best learning method for anyone.

All the tips I presented in the previous section did work for me—and for a few other people I know—but there is no magic formula that would suit everyone.

As I mentioned in the Preface, I know that each of us has a different background and follows a different path, but I wanted to say loud and clear that you don't need to have to be a graduate in IT to begin with Google Apps Script nor do you have to spend hours learning rules and conventions. Practice will make it easier everyday and motivation will give you enough energy to complete your projects, from simple ones to more ambiguous ones.

Summary

This chapter has given an overview of the many resources available to improve your learning experience. There are certainly more that I don't know of but as I already mentioned a few times before, we have powerful search engines in our browsers to help us.

We also have to keep in mind that Google Apps Script, as explained in this book, will probably be different as compared to what it will be in a couple of years. The last chapter will explain future evolution and development perspectives.

9
Conclusion

If you have reached this part of the book, I would assume you have read eight chapters and have quite a good view of what you can do with Google Apps Script. However, you have to know that all this is just a part of it—a small part actually.

I did present a few examples of data exchange between different Google services (docs and spreadsheets, Gmail and docs, and so on), but there is definitely much more to explore. This book could easily have over 500 pages without too much effort, but as the title states, this book just provides a few samples to help you to get started.

Development perspectives

Although I didn't mention all the presently available possibilities, there are quite a few. Google Apps Script is an evolving toolbox; the developers' team is still at work to expand its possibilities and application fields.

If you're curious, you should have a look at the release notes on the **Release Notes** page (`https://developers.google.com/apps-script/releases/`) they update every month, and you'll get a pretty good idea of what they've already accomplished and the number of issues they have fixed. I read it regularly, and I must say that I'm often quite impressed.

Google's secrets

Now if you want to be even more impressed, go have a look at the issue tracker page (`https://code.google.com/p/google-apps-script-issues/issues/list`). This is not only the place to drop the issues you are met with—although it is good to know and very useful to read as well—but it is also the place where users can place their enhancement requests.

Also, there are so many enhancement requests in so many fields that I guess they will probably never accept and implement all of them. However, I know they are very attentive to it and consider each of them most seriously, and evaluate their usefulness and feasibility. I know that we are going to be surprised by the numerous features they will add in the coming months, not to mention in the coming years!

I said earlier that learning Google Apps Script is a never-ending process, but I'm sure that developing it is even more endless.

Personal point of view

I guess that a combination of circumstances and opportunities has made me a Google Apps Script addict, but maybe in different circumstances, I could have learned a different language. Life is not always a matter of choice, but I must say that I'm really happy about this coincidence! It makes me feel like I am part of a really modern movement, something unique to our present environment.

Google Apps Script could not have existed in the 80s, nor even in the early 2000s. Computer technology was not powerful enough.

That feeling of modernity is actually quite pleasant, at least as far as computer science is concerned. Unfortunately, not everything in our modern world is so alluring, but that's another story.

My only hope when writing the final words in this small book is that I have given a few people the desire to go further with Google Apps Script and help them get enough self-confidence to start their own project.

Index

Thank you for buying
Google Apps Script for Beginners

About Packt Publishing

Packt, pronounced 'packed', published its first book *"Mastering phpMyAdmin for Effective MySQL Management"* in April 2004 and subsequently continued to specialize in publishing highly focused books on specific technologies and solutions.

Our books and publications share the experiences of your fellow IT professionals in adapting and customizing today's systems, applications, and frameworks. Our solution based books give you the knowledge and power to customize the software and technologies you're using to get the job done. Packt books are more specific and less general than the IT books you have seen in the past. Our unique business model allows us to bring you more focused information, giving you more of what you need to know, and less of what you don't.

Packt is a modern, yet unique publishing company, which focuses on producing quality, cutting-edge books for communities of developers, administrators, and newbies alike. For more information, please visit our website: www.packtpub.com.

Writing for Packt

We welcome all inquiries from people who are interested in authoring. Book proposals should be sent to author@packtpub.com. If your book idea is still at an early stage and you would like to discuss it first before writing a formal book proposal, contact us; one of our commissioning editors will get in touch with you.

We're not just looking for published authors; if you have strong technical skills but no writing experience, our experienced editors can help you develop a writing career, or simply get some additional reward for your expertise.

PUBLISHING

Google Maps JavaScript API Cookbook

ISBN: 978-1-84969-882-5   Paperback: 316 pages

Over 50 recipes to help you create web maps and GIS web applications using the Google Maps JavaScript API

1. Add to your website's functionality by utilizing Google Maps' power

2. Full of code examples and screenshots for practical and efficient learning

3. Empowers you to build your own mapping application from the ground up

Google Visualization API Essentials

ISBN: 978-1-84969-436-0   Paperback: 252 pages

Make sense of your data: make it visual with the Google Visualization API

1. Wrangle all sorts of data into a visual format, without being an expert programmer

2. Visualize new or existing spreadsheet data through charts, graphs, and maps

3. Full of diagrams, core concept explanations, best practice tips, and links to working book examples

Please check **www.PacktPub.com** for information on our titles

Instant Google Compute Engine

ISBN: 978-1-84969-700-2   Paperback: 60 pages

A quick guide to managing and operating your personal Cloud infrastructure using Google Compute Engine

1. Learn something new in an Instant! A short, fast, focused guide delivering immediate results

2. Learn how to use Google Compute Engine for your own projects

3. Quickly get started using virtual machines on Google Compute Engine

Google Apps: Mastering Integration and Customization

ISBN: 978-1-84969-216-8   Paperback: 268 pages

Scale your applications and projects onto the cloud with Google Apps

1. This is the English language translation of: Integrer Google Apps dans le SI, copyright Dunod, Paris, 2010

2. The quickest way to migrate to Google Apps - enabling you to get on with tasks

3. Overcome key challenges of Cloud Computing using Google Apps

Please check **www.PacktPub.com** for information on our titles

29292013R00101

Made in the USA
San Bernardino, CA
19 January 2016